# BEAUTIFUL PICTURES

## FROM THE GALLERY OF PHINANCE

*Beautiful Pictures*
*from the Gallery of Phinance*

Printed in the United States of America


For information, address the publishers:
New Classics Library
Post Office Box 1618
Gainesville, Georgia 30503 USA
Phone: 800-336-1618, 770-536-0309
Fax: 770-536-2514
E-mail address for products: customerservice@elliottwave.com
E-mail address for comments: bb@elliottwave.com
Web site: www.elliottwave.com


New Classics Library is the book publishing division of
Elliott Wave International, Inc.

ISBN: 0-932750-60-5

Library of Congress Catalog Control Number: 2003108260

# BEAUTIFUL PICTURES

## FROM THE GALLERY OF PHINANCE

BY ROBERT R. PRECHTER, JR.

New Classics Library

## *Acknowledgments*

Rachel Webb handled the toughest part of this book's physical production, which was the illustrations. Sally Webb executed the final layout, which was a challenge, and Darrell King, Marc Benejan and Roberta Machcinski produced the quite stylish jacket.

## Table of Contents

# AUTHOR'S NOTE

Mathematicians recognize that the stock market is a fractal but only in the sense that the irregularity of fluctuation is the same regardless of scale. In the 1930s, R.N. Elliott observed that the stock market is a *specific* fractal and named it the Wave Principle. As defined in *The Wave Principle of Human Social Behavior* (1999), the stock market fractal is robust, meaning that it has certain specificities of form as well as quantitative variations. One intriguing question is whether those variations also adhere to specificities. In other words, are they random, or do they have recognizable mathematical relationships?

This book investigates some price and time properties of fifth Elliott waves at Cycle and Supercycle degree, primarily the ones that ended simultaneously in 2000. The first chart in Chapter 5, which I initially drew by hand in April 2000, kicked off this project. I was continually amazed at how much more was there to discover. I hope you will come to share that feeling as you wend your way through this gallery of exquisite natural forms.

Obviously, the exercises undertaken for this book could go on forever. There are countless other waves to investigate at equal and smaller degrees. Due to the complexity of investigating, graphing and coordinating wave relationships, I do not plan a sequel. If I really had time on my hands, I would examine these waves in light of my 1977 study, "The Hidden Similarity of Two Wave Forms," which is reprinted in *Market Analysis for the New Millennium* (2002). Perhaps you will find the time to extend these efforts. By the way, I did all these calculations myself, and no one has checked them. If you find any errors, please let me know.

Most of this book was finished by late 2001, to which point many of the charts are updated. The delay in final printing was due to a rush of other projects, including *Conquer the Crash* and *Pioneering Studies in Socionomics*. Ironically, as this book finally goes to press in July 2003, the Dow has spent a year testing and then recovering from last summer's low. It is back above 9000, within 20% of where it was when I began these studies and well within the range of the post-peak prices through 2001 displayed on the graphs in Chapters 5 through 12. So any practical value that these studies possess (see Postscript) remains intact.

The most impressive illustrations in this book are marked with a "blue ribbon." If you are pressed for time, you can turn to those graphs and get the best of what is here. But to reap the full rewards in this book, you should sit back, get comfortable and take the full guided tour.

## Man of the Millennium

Next year when the millennium really ends, we would love to see Leonardo Fibonacci [of Pisa (c.1175 - c.1240)] at least make the list of contenders for the real Man of the Millennium. Without Fibonacci, there would have been no Gutenberg, Newton or Einstein because Fibonacci was the one who introduced the Hindu-Arabic numeral system, with its zero, to the west. As Joseph Gies wrote in *Leonard of Pisa*, Fibonacci "started a revolution in mathematics that is still going on seven and a half centuries later." As a pure mathematician, Fibonacci was 300 years ahead of his time. Of course, the really intriguing aspect to us is the Fibonacci sequence because its implications have only started to come to light. For this reason, he will probably be best remembered at the end of the *next* millennium.

— *The Elliott Wave Financial Forecast*,
January 7, 2000*

---

\* Five trading days before waves v, (v), ⓥ, 5, (5), ⑤, V, (V) and Ⓜ ended in the Dow.

# INTRODUCTION

## The Elliott Wave Fractal

A fractal is a self-similar or self-affine object. It looks like itself — to one degree or another — regardless of the scale at which you observe it. In the 1930s, Ralph Nelson Elliott discovered that the record of stock prices is a fractal. More important, he demonstrated that it is a *specific* fractal with a definite form, though it varies quantitatively. Figure 0-1 shows several iterations of one expression of an Elliott wave.

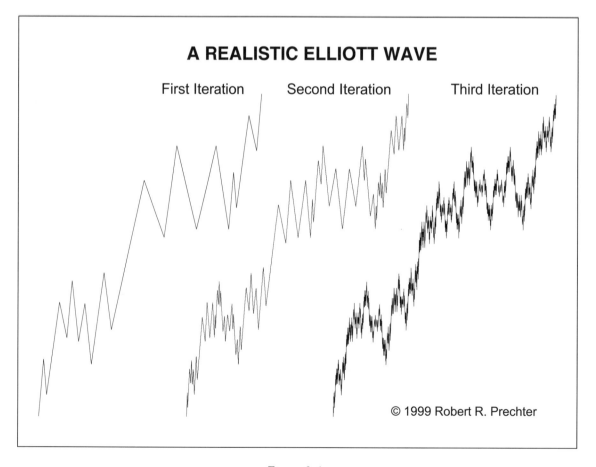

*Figure 0-1*

As I described in *The Wave Principle of Human Social Behavior*, records of financial market prices appear to be a special type of fractal that is typically found in the context of life forms, which it variously permeates (as in bronchial, cardiovascular and nervous systems) or regulates (as in growth patterns). I call it "robust" to designate a fractal that has both a *fixed quality of form*, like self-identical fractals such as nesting squares, as well as a *variable quantitative aspect*, like indefinite fractals such as clouds and seacoasts.

The purpose of the studies in this book is to explore whether there are quantitative specificities in Elliott waves. We discover that the "roughness" in the stock market — its supposed "irregularity" — may be an artifact of insufficient observation. At least, the quantitative specificities of mass cooperative behavior are increasingly revealed to be more numerous than generally assumed.

## The Fibonacci Sequence and the Wave Principle

The Fibonacci sequence is 1, 1, 2, 3, 5, 8, 13, 21, 34, 55, and so on. It begins with the number 1, and each successive term is the sum of the previous two. The limit ratio between adjacent terms is .618034..., an irrational number variously called the "golden mean" and "divine proportion," but in this century more succinctly "phi" ($\phi$). A "golden section" is a line split into Fibonacci proportion, as follows:

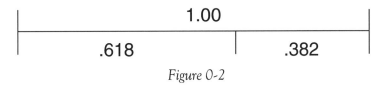

Figure 0-2

You will see quite a few golden sections in this book.

Both the Fibonacci sequence and the Fibonacci ratio appear ubiquitously in natural forms ranging from the geometry of the DNA molecule to the physiology of plants and animals to patterns of human mentation. For examples, see Chapters 3, 11 and 12 in *The Wave Principle of Human Social Behavior*.

Elliott's publisher, renowned investment advisor Charles Collins, first realized that the Wave Principle is connected to the Fibonacci sequence and communicated that fact to Elliott.[1] After researching the subject to the small extent possible at the time, Elliott presented the final unifying conclusion of his theory in 1940,[2] explaining that the progress of waves has the same mathematical base as so many phenomena of life.

The Fibonacci sequence governs the numbers of waves that form the movement of aggregate stock prices in an expansion upon the underlying 5-3 relationship. Figure 0-3 shows the progression. The simplest expression of a corrective wave is a straight-line decline. The simplest expression of a motive wave is a straight-line advance. A complete cycle is two lines. At the next degree of complexity, the corresponding numbers are 3, 5 and 8. This sequence continues to infinity.

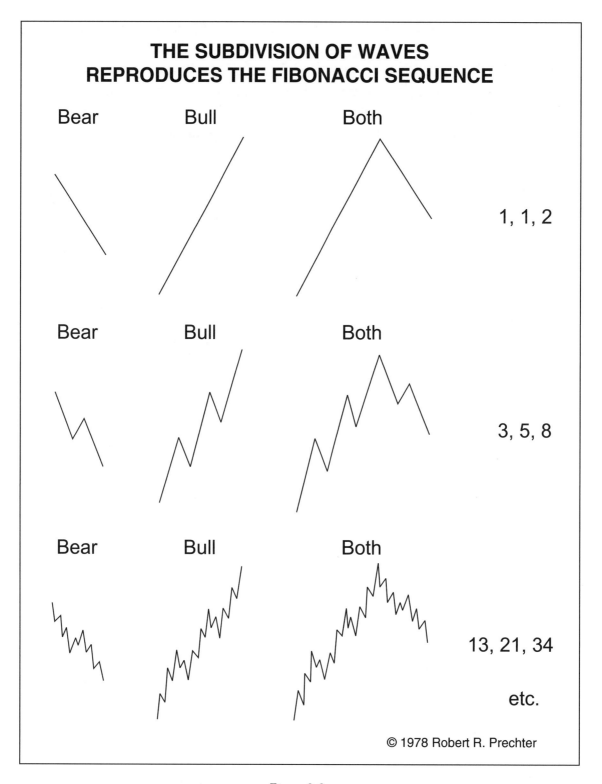

*Figure 0-3*

## Notation and Nomenclature

Waves are categorized by degree. The degree of a wave is determined by its size and position relative to component, adjacent and encompassing waves. Elliott named nine degrees of waves, from the smallest discernible on a graph of hourly stock prices to the largest he could assume existed from the data then available. The illustrations in this book label only three degrees of waves, which in order of increasing size are called Primary, Cycle and Supercycle. Primary waves link together to form Cycle waves, which link together to form Supercycle waves and so on, to Grand Supercycle waves and higher. Though not labeled in this book, Primary waves in turn subdivide into Intermediate waves, which subdivide into Minor waves, and so on as well. Primary waves are labeled with Arabic numerals in circles, such as ③, Cycle waves are labeled with Roman numerals, such as **III**, and Supercycle waves are labeled with Roman numerals in parentheses, such as **(III)**.

In the foregoing studies, the symbol φ stands for any value that attains or approximates .618 or its inverse 1.618 or any fraction composed of adjacent Fibonacci numbers. The symbol $φ^2$ stands for any value that attains or approximates .382 or its inverse 2.618 or any fraction composed of alternate Fibonacci numbers.

For expanded discussions of the details of the Wave Principle and the Fibonacci sequence, please see Chapters 1 through 4 of *Elliott Wave Principle* and Chapters 1 and 3 of *The Wave Principle of Human Social Behavior*.

---

[1] Prechter, Robert R., Ed. (1980/1994). "A Biography of R.N. Elliott." *R.N. Elliott's Masterworks*. Gainesville GA: New Classics Library, p. 56

[2] Elliott, Ralph Nelson. (1940, October 1). "The basis of the wave principle." Republished: (1980/1994). *R.N. Elliott's Masterworks — The Definitive Collection*. Prechter, Robert R. (Ed.). Gainesville, GA: New Classics Library.

# Chapter 1

# Formal Self-Affinity Between Two Fifth-Wave Expressions of the Elliott Wave Fractal

The investigations in this book hinge on the conclusion — and also support the conclusion — that the bull market that began in 1974 and the larger one that began in 1932 ended in the first quarter of 2000. I believe this conclusion to be a good bet for many reasons, not the least of which is certain self-affine wave characteristics such as those displayed in this and subsequent chapters.

### *Figures 1-1 and 1-2:*

### An Intriguing Correlation

Figure 1-1 shows two price series. Figure 1-2 shows the two series overlaid. One of them is a recent multi-year period in the Dow Jones Industrial Average. Before I reveal what the other series is, wouldn't you agree that the two series appear closely correlated? An economist would be excited, one would think, to have a data series that correlated this closely with the stock market. Let's find out what it is.

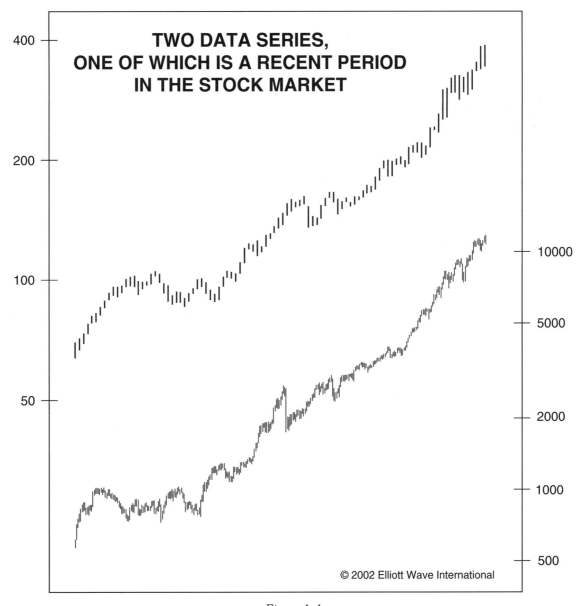

*Figure 1-1*

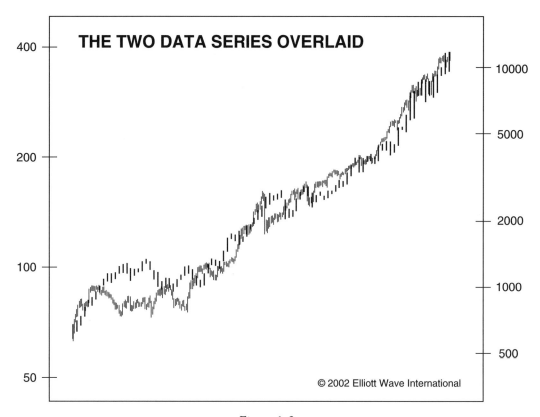

*Figure 1-2*

## Figure 1-3:

## Cousins

Figure 1-3 shows the "Grand Supercycle" degree uptrend in the U.S. stock market that began circa 1784. (For a discussion of the data sources, see Chapter 13.) It subdivides into five waves of Supercycle degree, labeled (I), (II), (III), (IV), (V), which in turn subdivide into Cycle degree waves labeled I, II, III, IV, V. This is the template from which we will investigate two waves of the same *number* (fifth) and *degree* (Cycle).

Only two fifth waves of this degree have detailed daily and intra-day price records, as recorded by the Dow Jones Industrial Average (DJIA): the 1921-1929 advance, which was wave **V** of (III), and the 1974-2000 advance, which was wave **V** of (V). These waves are highlighted in bold on the graph.

Look back at Figures 1-1 and 1-2 and realize that *both* plots are of the DJIA. In fact, they are the monthly ranges of the highlighted portions of Figure 1-3, plotted so that they take up the same space on the page. Although the two waves are quantitatively different in terms both of duration (8.1 years and 25.1 years) and extent (596.5% gain vs. 1929.6% gain), their nuances of *form* — representing the progression of mass psychology — are strikingly similar.

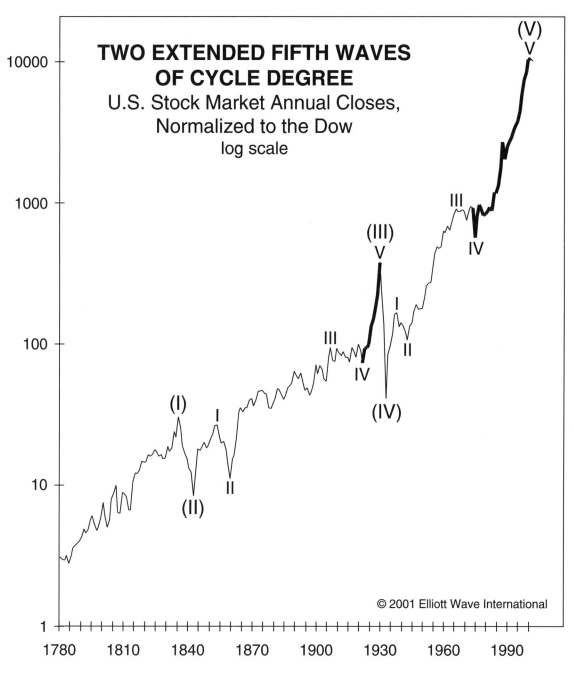

*Figure 1-3*

**Figure 1-4:**

## The Formal Affinity of Two Cycle-Degree Fifth Waves

Figure 1-4 displays the same data but with the 1920s bull market depicted by the weekly range so that the data frequency of the two plots more closely match. While these two bull markets subdivide into the requisite five Primary waves (marked with numbers in circles), there is much more to their similarity than that. The notes on the graph detail some of the similarities in form between these two Cycle-degree fifth waves, as follows:

- Wave ① is a steep jump.
- Wave ② consists of two downward moves, one long and one short.
- Wave ② is followed by a deep decline that bottoms just slightly above the low of wave ②.
- Wave ② and its test are associated with economic recession(s).
- From that point forward, wave ③ is a steep ascent.
- Wave ④ begins with a crash.
- Wave ④ includes a new all-time high.
- Wave ④ ends above the crash low.
- The end of wave ④ coincides with the start of an economic recession.
- Wave ⑤ is extended.
- Wave ⑤ starts slowly and then accelerates.
- A consolidation precedes the final high.
- The portion of the wave following the test of the low of wave ② appears upwardly "stretched" compared to most impulses. Its corrections are exceptionally shallow, including a "running correction" (see *Elliott Wave Principle*, p.46-48) for wave ④.

Even many of the quantitative aspects of these two waves are similar. Several of the waves and turning points share approximately the same length, height and/or width. Overall, the 1974-2000 advance produced **3.2** times the percentage gain of the 1921-1929 advance in **3.1** times the time. (1929.6%/596.5% = **3.2**; 25.1 yrs./8.1 yrs. = **3.1**.) In other words, these two bull markets' net non-compounded percentage gains over time are essentially identical. (For more on this theme, see Chapter 12.)

The social results of these psychological progressions are also quite similar. These two periods shared a stock mania, a real estate boom, easy credit, a preoccupation with finance, drug prohibition, a relatively peaceful world scene and middle-of-the-road politics. Observe that in each case, the corrections for waves ② and ④ produced recessions. They appeared at nearly the same times as well. In the early 1990s, extensive layoffs and the biggest collapse in S&P earnings since the early 1940s dogged the economy right through 1993, even though the Bureau of Economic Research declared the recession "officially" over in 1991.

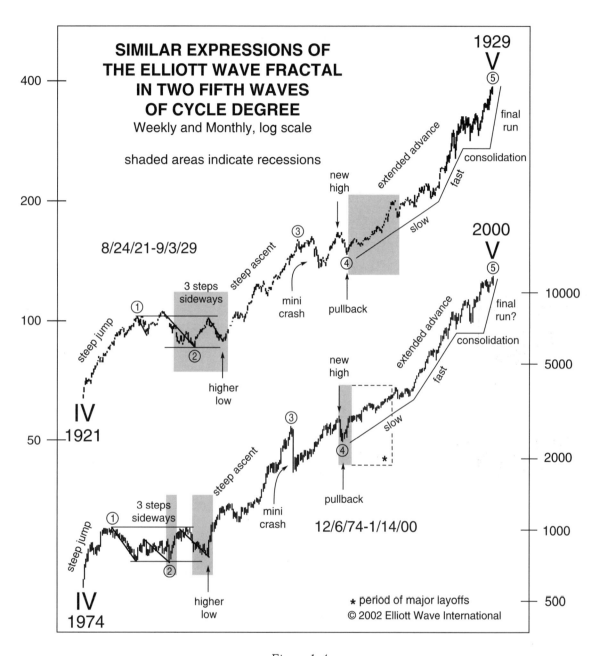

**SIMILAR EXPRESSIONS OF
THE ELLIOTT WAVE FRACTAL
IN TWO FIFTH WAVES
OF CYCLE DEGREE**
Weekly and Monthly, log scale

shaded areas indicate recessions

8/24/21-9/3/29

12/6/74-1/14/00

★ period of major layoffs
© 2002 Elliott Wave International

*Figure 1-4*

The numerous similarities cited above are not likely coincidence. If time were irrelevant to human behavior (which, in terms of generating social forms, it probably is), the two data series would be a record of essentially the same social experience. While a single instance of close similarity between two waves of the same number and degree may not be enough for generalizing, we might at least begin to suspect that fifth Elliott waves of Cycle degree share certain quantitative aspects of form, which in turn have similar results in social action. This particular form may be an expression of how mass psychology progresses in a Cycle degree fifth wave whose fifth sub-wave is extended (i.e., significantly larger than at least one of the other motive waves in the structure). If so, then we may ultimately suggest that the socionomic hypothesis[1] be refined to take into account wave number and degree as aspects of causality with respect to nuances of social result. We already know that different wave numbers have different "personalities" in terms of market and thus psychological behavior (see *Elliott Wave Principle*, p. 76), so it is hardly a stretch to propose that the character of resulting social action differs accordingly.

Think about how different these periods were in terms of technology, communication, world events and political status. The U.S. was a farming country in the 1920s. It was a financial center in the 1990s. People communicated by telegram and letter in 1929, by email and cell phone in 2000. People read newspapers in the 1920s, and they watched satellite television in the 1990s. The U.S. was emerging from political isolationism in the 1920s, and in the 1990s, it was the only world-class political power. What is undeniably the *same* in the two periods, though, is the psychological progression within society, which is what Elliott waves in the stock market depict. The general level of technology is irrelevant to those progressions.

## 1920s Redux

As remarkable as it is that the advance of 1974-2000 mirrored that of 1921-1929 so closely, it is of more scientific import that practitioners of the Wave Principle *predicted* an affinity between the two periods. From as far back as the 1970s, I have been steadfast — as was my co-author A.J. Frost — in identifying the rise dating from 1974 as the fifth wave of a Supercycle degree uptrend and thus a "cousin" of the bull markets of 1921-1929, 1829-1835 and 1716-1720, which were also fifth waves of Supercycle-degree uptrends. For this reason, we forecast that the bull market due to emerge from the 1974 and 1982 lows would be, in a number of ways, *akin to that of the 1920s.* Below is a chronicle of early commentary on this subject, from well before any such similarities were apparent.

"...the current Cycle bull market should resemble a simpler structure and a shorter time period such as the 1932-37 and 1921-29 markets. [L]ike the nine years of 'work' under the 100 level prior to the bull market of the 1920s, the last fifth Cycle wave, the Dow has currently concluded thirteen years of work under the 1000 level. And, as the Dow's orthodox peak in 1928 occurred at 296 according to Elliott's interpretation, the next peak is estimated at about the same relative level, although an extended flat correction could carry the averages into even higher ground temporarily." — *Elliott Wave Principle*, November 1978

"[The second wave labeling] fits the idea that the Kondratieff Wave plateau has just begun, a period of economic stability and soaring stock prices. Parallel with late 1921. [The first wave labeling] fits the idea that the Kondratieff Wave plateau is partly over. Parallel with 1923. ...An interesting observation with regard to this target is that it parallels the 1920s, when...the market soared almost nonstop to an intraday peak of 383.00. As with this fifth wave, such a move would finish off not only a Cycle but a Supercycle advance." — *The Elliott Wave Theorist*, September 1982

"Turn your mind to 1924." — *The Elliott Wave Theorist*, November 1982

"The 1920s bull market was a fifth wave of a *third* Supercycle wave, while Cycle wave V is the fifth wave of a *fifth* Supercycle wave. ...Expect a swift and persistent advance with short corrections as opposed to long rolling advances with evenly spaced corrective phases." — *The Elliott Wave Theorist*, April 1983

"Is my Elliott-based expectation of a 400% gain in 5-8 years a wild one? It appears to be, when compared to recent history. But not when compared to 1921-1929, a 500% gain in 8 years, or 1932-1937, a 400% gain in 5 years." — *The Elliott Wave Theorist*, August 1983

This advance orientation to the 1920s experience was virtually unique. As you may glean from one of the quotes above, the only other approach to stock market forecasting that one could have used to come generally to the same conclusion is the Kondratieff monetary/economic cycle, and I am aware of only two other students of the cycle who did so.[2] Still, the Wave Principle is the only approach to market analysis that can provide the insights in Figure 1-4 because it is the only model in which form takes precedence over periodicity. Approaches in which time rules (such as with the "time cycles" approach, the Decennial Pattern, the Presidential Election cycle, etc.) are not attuned to such subtleties. Finally, observe that in order to predict the bull market's affinity to the 1920s, *one had to predict a great bull market in the first place*. This dual forecast was possible because of the Wave Principle.

---

[1] See p. 16 of *The Wave Principle of Human Social Behavior*.
[2] Peter Eliades of *Stockmarket Cycles* and P.Q. Wall of *The P.Q. Wall Forecast*.

*Chapter 2*

## *Quantitative Self-Affinity Among Three Fifth-Wave Expressions of the Elliott Wave Fractal*

To expand our perspective, we will now investigate a third major fifth wave that sports an extended fifth sub-wave. This new addition, plotted at the top of Figure 2-1, is Supercycle wave (V) from 1932 to 2000, plotted to cover the same space on the page as the other two waves. Of course, this wave ended concurrently with its final component of one lesser degree, wave V. To see where these three waves fit into the Grand Supercycle advance from 1784, refer to Figure 1-3. Although these three waves are vastly different in terms of percentage gain and duration, they share certain quantitative aspects.

### *Figure 2-1:*

### The Similar Positions of Wave Three and Four's Endpoints

The most striking shared aspect of these waves is the nearly identical placement of the endpoints of waves three and four. In all three cases, these waves appear to terminate at nearly the same price and time with respect to the length of the entire wave. Let's take a closer look, beginning with the position of the third-wave peaks.

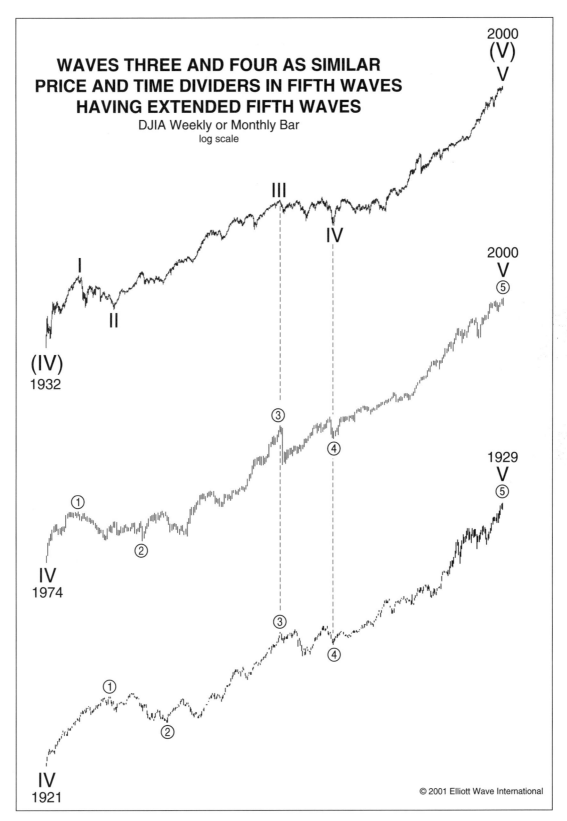

*Figure 2-1*

*Figure 2-2:*

## Wave Three as an Equality Time Divider (in Years)

Two weeks after the all-time high in the Dow in January 2000, *The Elliott Wave Theorist* published Figures 2-2 and 2-3, noting that the simultaneous end of waves ⑤ and V was timed so that the peaks of waves ③ and III respectively split waves V and (V) into equal Fibonacci numbers of years. Figure 2-4 reveals that the peak of wave ③ in the 1920s occurred at the same relative position.

As published in *The Elliott Wave Theorist* of February 2000

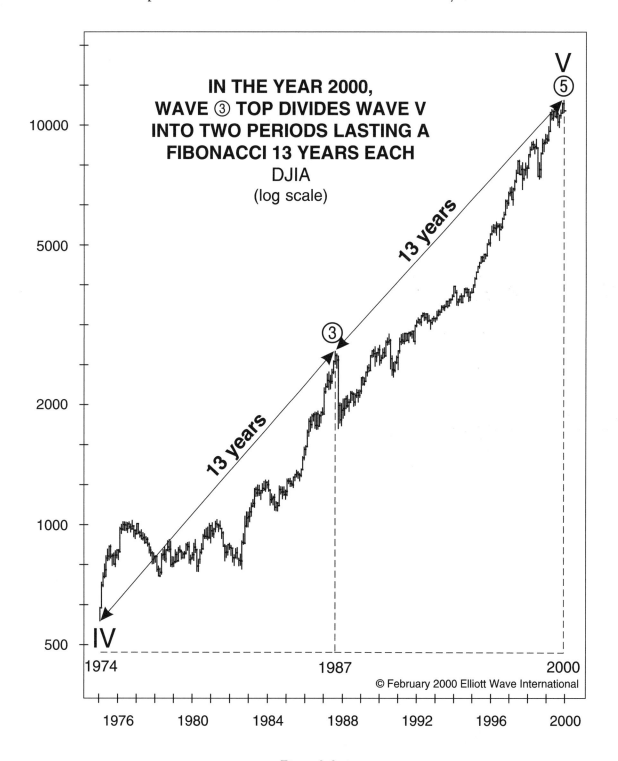

Figure 2-2

As published in *The Elliott Wave Theorist* of February 2000

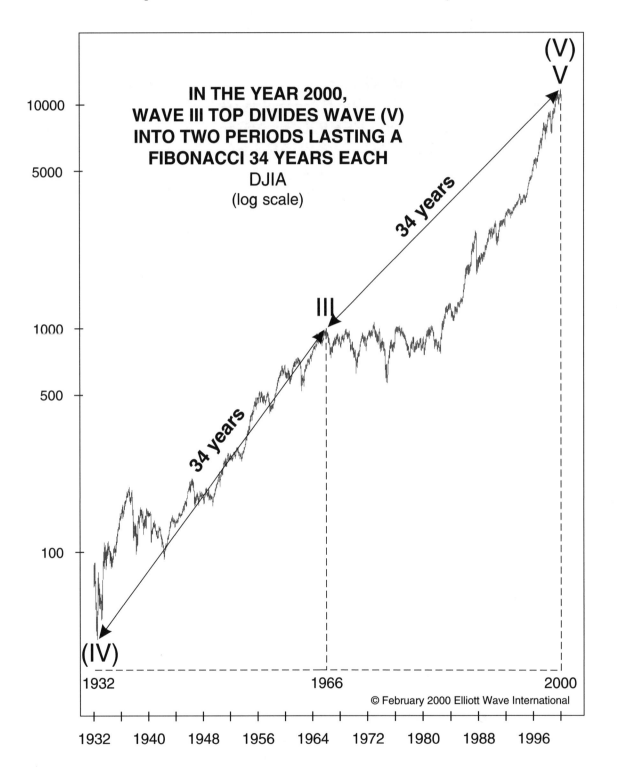

Figure 2-3

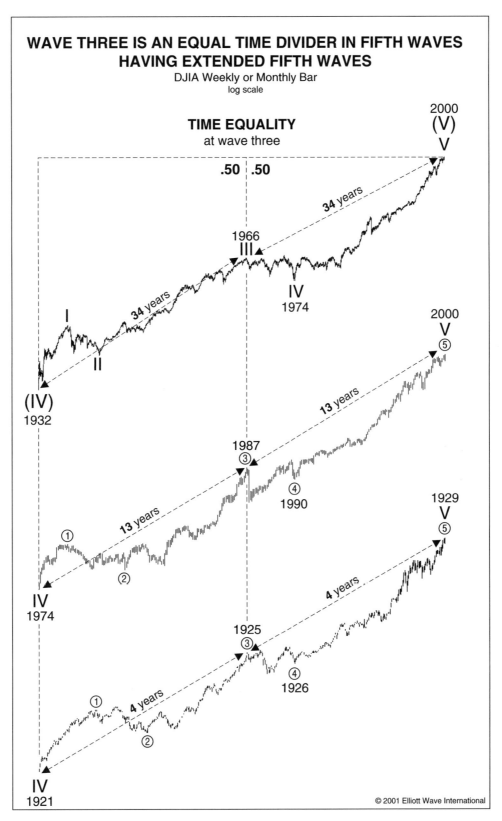

Figure 2-4

*Figure 2-5:*

## Wave Four as a Fibonacci Time Divider (in Years)

Now let's look at the position of the fourth-wave troughs. As you can see in Figure 2-5, wave four, like wave three, occurs at the same time relative to the length of each whole wave, but this time, the splits create not equal sections but Fibonacci sections. In each case, the duration up to the low of wave four is $\phi$ times the total duration. Further, by definition, the duration of wave five is $\phi$ times the duration up to the low of wave four and $\phi^2$ times the total duration. Specifically, in the bottom graph, wave ⑤ covers **3 out of 8** years (**3/8**); in the middle graph, wave ⑤ covers **10 out of 26** years (**5/13**); in the top graph, wave V covers **26 out of 68** years (**13/34**), a $\phi^2$ relationship in each case. The periods preceding the end of wave four cover **5 out of 8** years (**5/8**), **8 out of 13** years (**8/13**) and **21 out of 34** years (**21/34**), respectively, a $\phi$ relationship in each case. The two periods to the right and left of the end of wave four, then, last **3 and 5** years (**3/5**) in the bottom graph, **10 and 16** years (**5/8**) in the middle graph, and **13 and 21** years (**13/21**) in the top graph, also a $\phi$ relationship in each case.

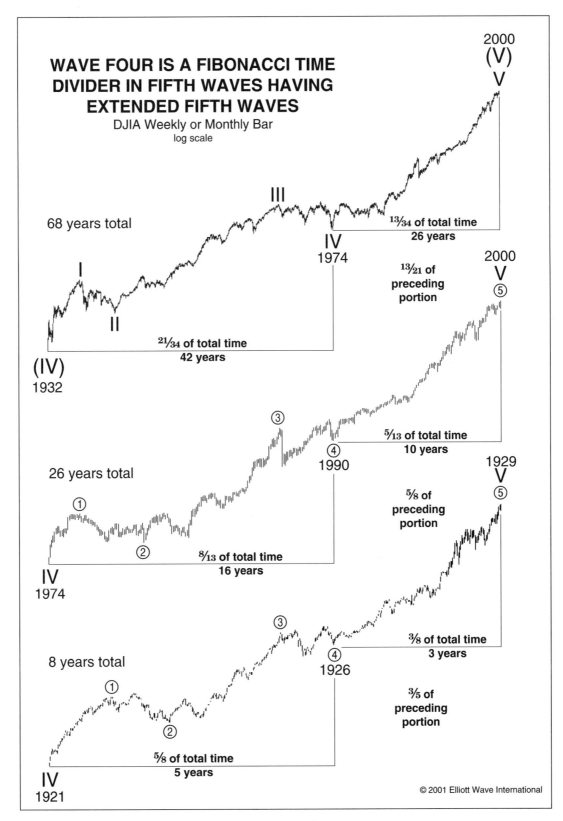

*Figure 2-5*

*Figure 2-6:*

## The Distinct Roles of Waves Three and Four

Figure 2-6 places these time observations for waves three and four in one illustration. Because all these waves have the same durational subdivisions and because those subdivisions are .50 and .618, I conclude that these events are guidelines pertaining to fifth waves in the stock market that contain extended fifth waves.

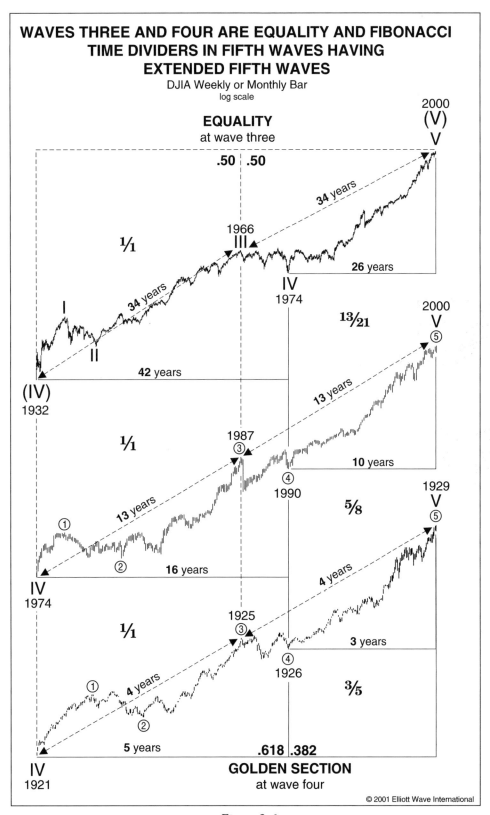

Figure 2-6

## Figure 2-7:

## The Wave Three Time Ratio in Days

Years are rough measurements of wave durations. How do the relationships appear when expressed more precisely in days?

Figure 2-7 shows the three wave divisions in terms of days. (See the end of Chapter 4 for an explanation of how days are counted.) The measurements are as follows:

*Top*: Wave III ends at 12,269 days out of 24,661 days, at the **.4975** division point.

*Middle*: Wave ③ ends at 4645 days out of 9170 days, at the **.5065** division point.

*Bottom*: Wave ③ ends at 1535 days out of 2932 days, at the **.5235** division point.

The ratios between the two sides of wave three are not precisely the same to the day. The range is .51 ±.013.

The middle graph includes notes on durations and ratios with respect to the two S&P peaks in 2000, about which we will learn more in Chapter 3. Using the March 24, 2000 peak in the S&P, the divisions of waves (V) and V at their third-wave peaks are .496 and .503, which both round to .50. Using the September 6, 2000 peak in the S&P, the divisions of waves (V) and V at their third-wave peaks are **.4928** and **.4938**, which are nearly identical. (See also Figure 10-7.)

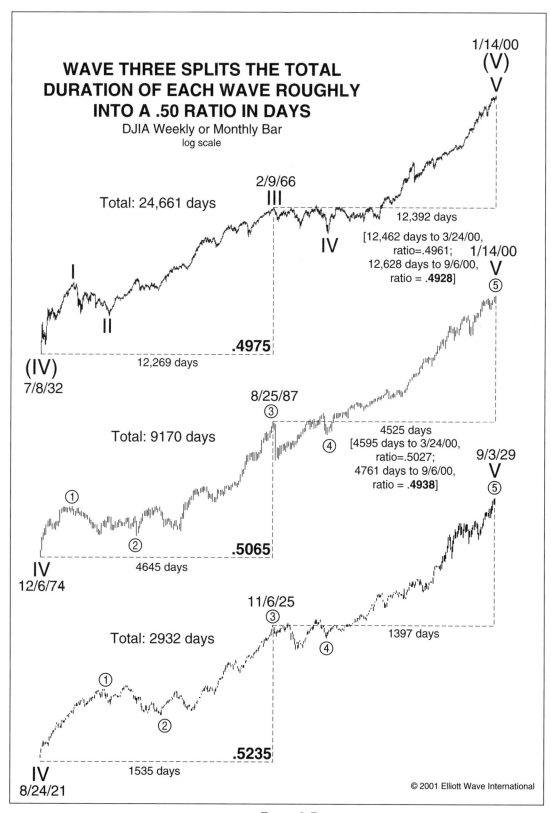

**WAVE THREE SPLITS THE TOTAL
DURATION OF EACH WAVE ROUGHLY
INTO A .50 RATIO IN DAYS**
DJIA Weekly or Monthly Bar
log scale

1/14/00
(V)
V

2/9/66
III

Total: 24,661 days

12,392 days
[12,462 days to 3/24/00,
ratio=.4961;
12,628 days to 9/6/00,
ratio = **.4928**]

IV

I

1/14/00
V
⑤

II

.4975
12,269 days

(IV)
7/8/32

8/25/87
③

Total: 9170 days

4525 days
[4595 days to 3/24/00,
ratio=.5027;
4761 days to 9/6/00,
ratio = **.4938**]

④

9/3/29
V
⑤

①

②

.5065
4645 days

IV
12/6/74

11/6/25
③

Total: 2932 days

1397 days

④

①

②

.5235
1535 days

IV
8/24/21

© 2001 Elliott Wave International

*Figure 2-7*

*Figure 2-8:*

**The Wave Four Time Ratio in Days**

Using wave four as a time divider, the measurements in days are as follows:

*Top:* Wave IV ends at 15,491 days out of 24,661 days, at the **.6282** division point.
*Middle:* Wave ④ ends at 5788 days out of 9170 days, at the **.6312** division point.
*Bottom:* Wave ④ ends at 1882 days out of 2932 days, at the **.6419** division point.

In these cases, then, the end of each wave four is a marker that not only divides its entire impulse wave into two sections of essentially the same relative duration but also does so to create very nearly a Fibonacci section at **.628-.642** of the whole, which is .635 ± .007, as shown in Figure 2-8.

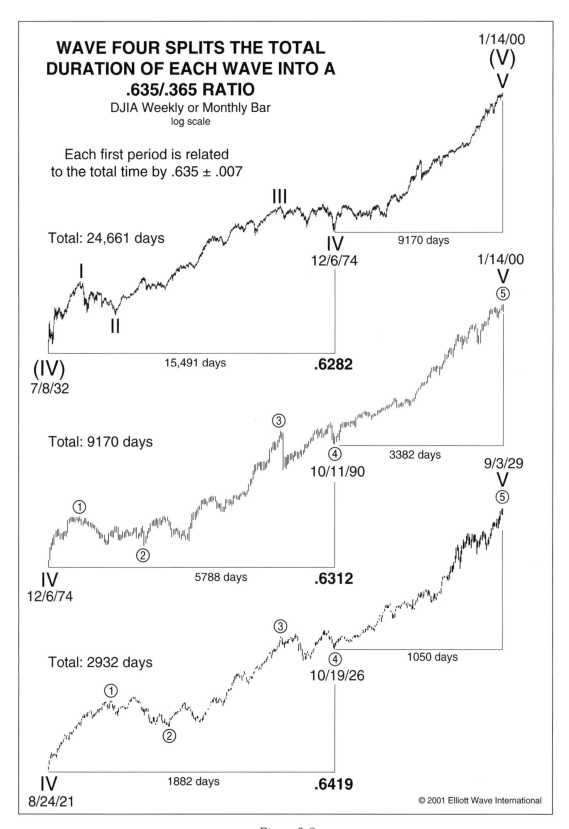

Figure 2-8

*Figure 2-9:*

## Cross-Relationships in the Durations of the Three Waves

The three waves depicted in the preceding graphs could have any individual durations and still sport the same ratio of subdivision at waves three and four. Actually, however, these three waves have similar ratios *between* their respective durations. The smallest wave lasts **.323** times the next larger, which lasts **.371** times the next larger, as you can see in Figure 2-9. Both of these numbers are close to $\phi^2$, being just below **1/3** and **3/8**, respectively. The market not only makes similar forms for its waves, but it may also be relating those forms to each other by Fibonacci fractions. Chapters 7, 10 and 11 will strengthen this case.

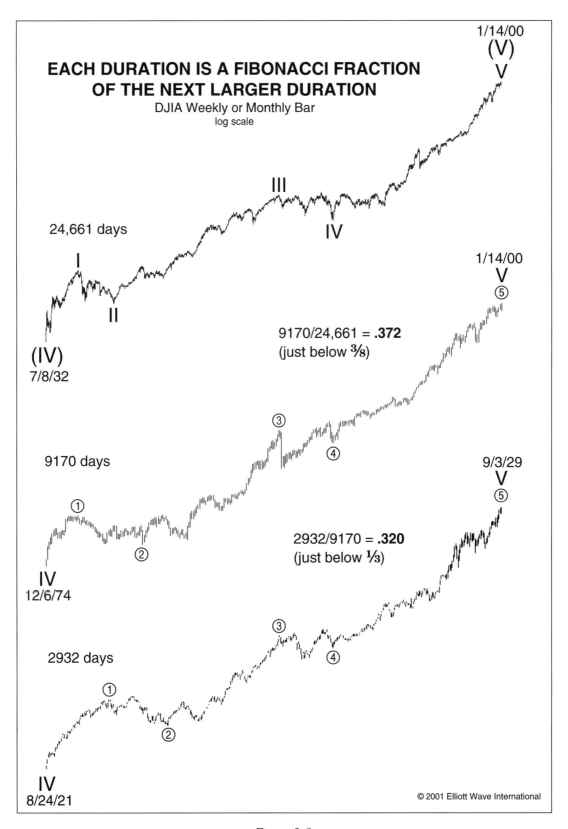

Figure 2-9

**Figure 2-10:**

## Wave Three as a Price Marker

Wave three appears to serve not only as a time marker but also as a price marker for these waves. On logarithmic scale, the price distance from the starting point of each wave up to the peak at the end of wave three is nearly the same in all three cases. Here are the exact measurements:

*Top*: Wave III ends at 2.998 in a log range of 1.615-4.069, at the **.563** division point.

*Middle*: Wave ③ ends at 3.435 in a log range of 2.762-4.069, at the **.515** division point.

*Bottom*: Wave ③ ends at 2.202 in a log range of 1.806-2.581, at the **.511** division point.

The end of each wave three, then, is a marker dividing the entire impulse wave into two sections at roughly the same point in terms of price logs, as you can see in Figure 2-10. Observe that in the two waves of the same degree, Cycle wave V (middle and bottom chart), the division is virtually identical at **.513** ±.002.

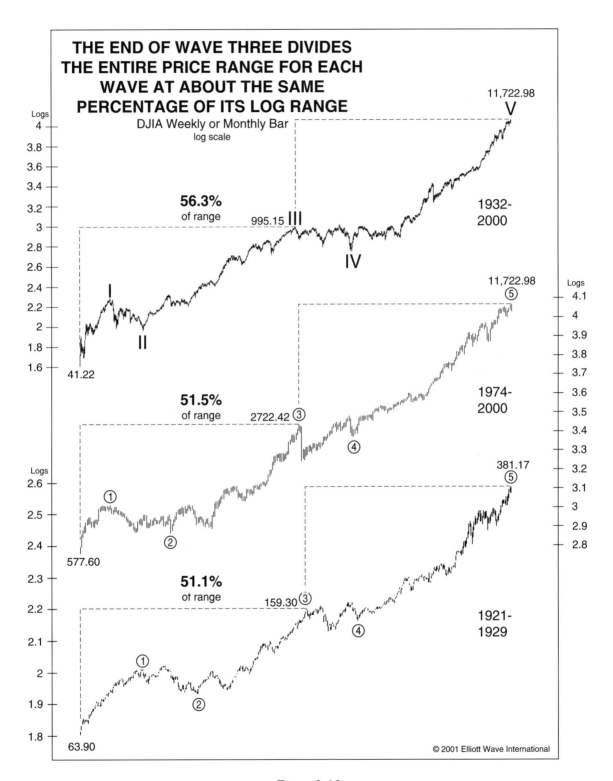

*Figure 2-10*

### Figure 2-11:

## Wave Four as a Price Marker

Wave four is also more than just a time marker in these waves; it is a price marker as well. On log scale, the price distance from the starting point of each wave up to the low at the end of wave four is virtually the same in all three cases. Here are the measurements:

*Top*: Wave IV ends at 2.762 in a log range of 1.615-4.069, it at the **.4672** division point.

*Middle*: Wave ④ ends at 3.374 in a log range of 2.762-4.069, at the **.4683** division point.

*Bottom*: Wave ④ ends at 2.163 in a log range of 1.806-2.581, at the **.4614** division point.

It follows, then, that the price distance of wave five is also virtually the same in all three cases. This means that the end of each wave four divides each entire impulse wave into two sections of the same relative height, expressed in logs of price, as you can see in Figure 2-11. That point is at **46.5%**, ± 0.4. The division points at waves IV in 1974 and ④ in 1990 (see top two charts) are very close to each other, at .4672 and .4683, respectively.

These divisions would have been identical (at .4660) had the Dow peaked 1.5 percent higher, at 11,895. This is almost precisely the number forecasted in *The Elliott Wave Theorist* in May 1998 for the ultimate top, as illustrated in Figure 3-7, based on a .618 relationship among the Dow's long term waves. As Figure 4-1 will show, the Dow opted to create an exact 5/8 relationship rather than an exact .618 relationship, slightly compromising what otherwise would have been identical points of subdivision by the ends of waves IV and ④.

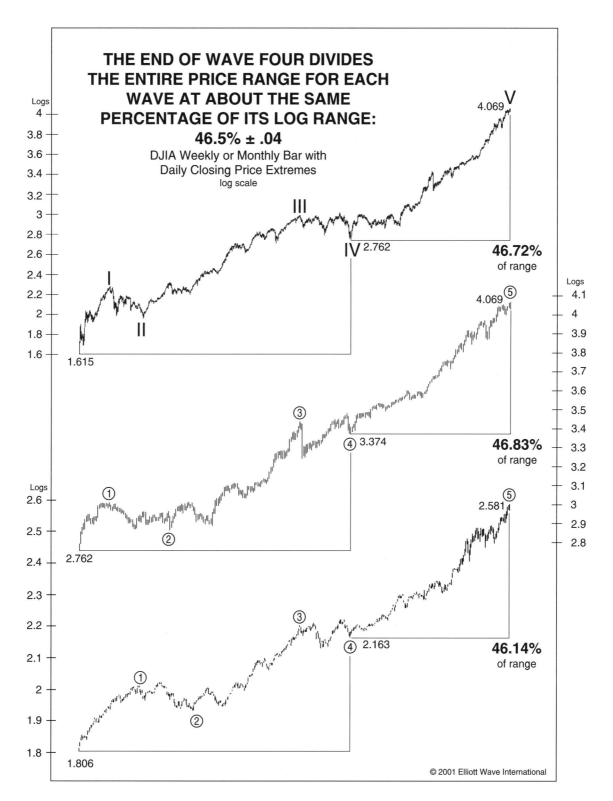

*Figure 2-11*

### Figure 2-12 and 2-13:

## Wave Four Overall as a 50 Percent Price Divider

As shown in the combined Figure, 2-12, neither the start nor the end of wave four marks precisely the 50 percent division point in terms of logs of price. It is the case, though, that the 50 percent division point comes *within* wave four every time, as you can see in Figure 2-13. We may have a new guideline, then, which is that in terms of price logs, wave four straddles the halfway point of an entire fifth wave in which the fifth wave is extended.

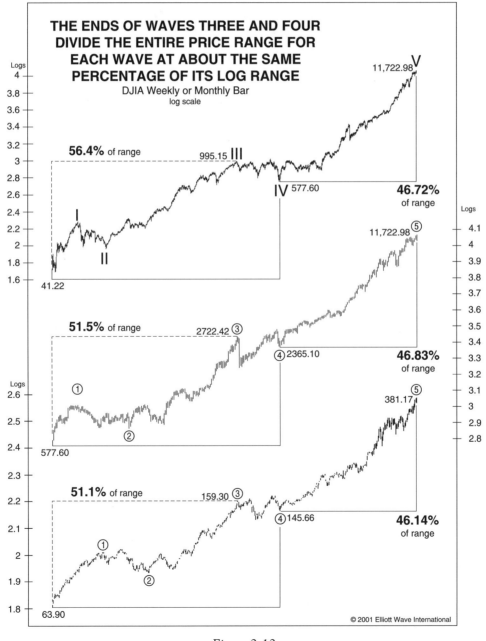

*Figure 2-12*

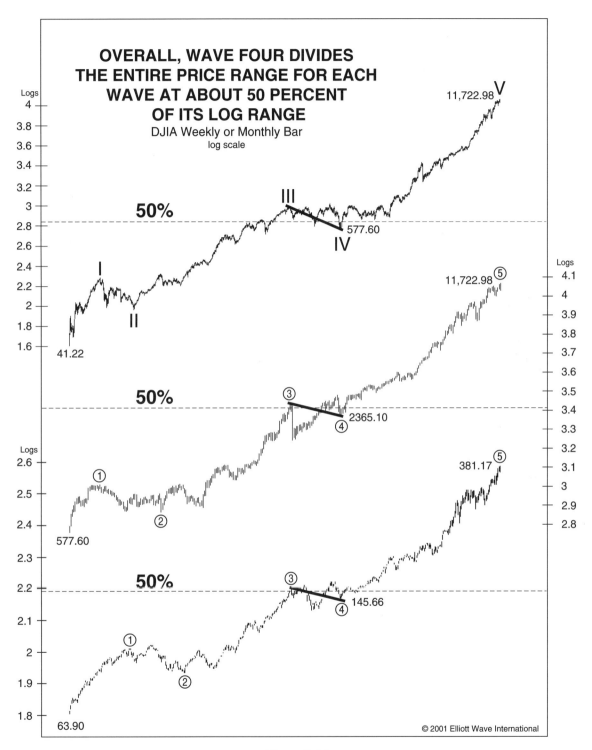

*Figure 2-13*

## *Figure 2-14:*

### Wave Four Is the Most Consistent Divider

While the end of wave three is an interesting divider, the end of wave four seems so far to be a more reliably precise one. Figure 2-14 shows that wave four in all three cases is both a price and time anchor for the entire wave. In other words, given any wave in the future that contains a double extension in waves three and five and which itself is the second extension of a double extension, we should be able well before wave five is over to project its end in both price and time to within a very tight range.

As we will see in Chapter 10, the extent of this precision, and our ability to predict, may be even greater when one of the fifth waves that we are assessing is a component of the other. In the next chapter, we will demonstrate that the positioning of wave four at a Fibonacci division point for all these waves is not the result of data mining but rather the application of an guideline formulated over half a century ago.

### A Hint of More Precise Self-Affinity between Waves V and (V) in Both Price and Time

Figure 1-4 showed that Cycle wave V of the 1920s mightily resembles Cycle wave V of 1974-2000. Figure 2-10 also implies a close affinity. Yet self-affinity typically refers not to various separate expressions of a type of fractal object but to the similarity of the *same* object at *different component degrees*. Figures 2-7, 2-8 and 2-11 show cases in which the closest similarity occurs between wave (V) *and its component*, wave V. Especially impressive is the position of the end of wave four:

— In terms of *price*, wave four subdivides these waves at the **.467** and **.468** points respectively, which are nearly identical.

— In terms of *time*, wave four subdivides these waves at the **.628** and **.631** points respectively, which are identical to two decimal places, at **.63**.

Chapters 7 and 10 will focus more closely upon Fibonacci relationships between waves (V) and V, the two largest waves of this set, the latter of which is a component of the former. As we will see later, when using the S&P's March 2000 high, the time relationships between these waves are actually perfect to the day. But first, we will cover some necessary background information and explore the price and time components of each of these waves.

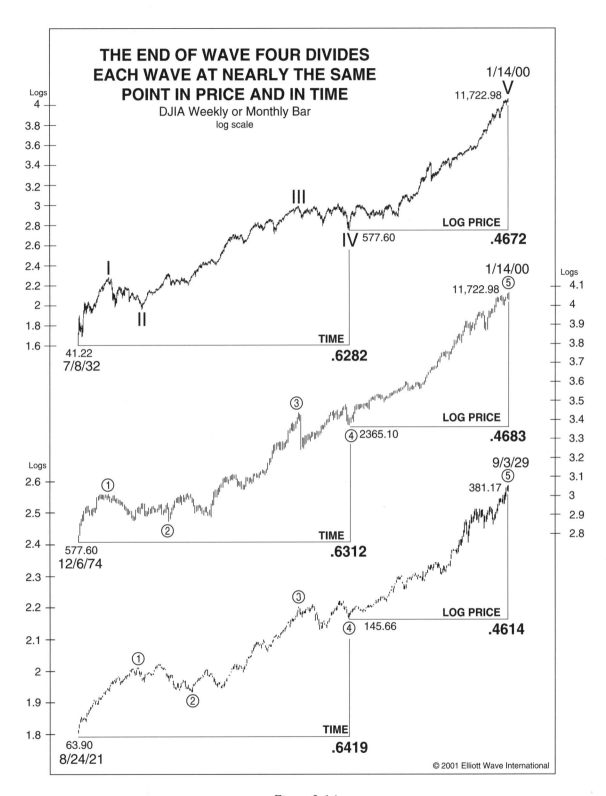

**THE END OF WAVE FOUR DIVIDES
EACH WAVE AT NEARLY THE SAME
POINT IN PRICE AND IN TIME**
DJIA Weekly or Monthly Bar
log scale

© 2001 Elliott Wave International

*Figure 2-14*

**Chapter 3**

# A Review of Pertinent Elliott Wave Measuring Guidelines

## Fifth Waves

Figure 3-1 shows some characteristics of an idealized Elliott wave. Supercycle wave (V) from 1932 and Cycle wave V from 1974 have progressed through the required stages, ending simultaneously in the first quarter of 2000. Both of these waves are *fifth* waves and as such have adhered to this description in *Elliott Wave Principle* (1978):

> **Fifth** waves – Fifth waves in stocks are always less dynamic than third waves in terms of breadth. They usually display a slower maximum speed of price change as well, although if a fifth wave is an extension, speed of price change in the third *of* the fifth can exceed that of the third wave. Even if a fifth wave extends, the fifth of the fifth will lack the dynamism that preceded it. During advancing fifth waves, optimism runs extremely high despite a narrowing of breadth.

Waves V and (V) both extended, so they had the exceptional dynamism associated with extensions, but breadth was relatively narrow, as required for a fifth wave. (See the discussions in Chapter 9 of *At the Crest of the Tidal Wave* and in the December 1999 issue of *The Elliott Wave Theorist*, reprinted in *View from the Top of the Grand Supercycle*.) This fact proves that Cycle wave V is properly labeled as a fifth wave, as it has been since before it even began.

# Elliott Wave Characteristics
© Prechter 1980/2001

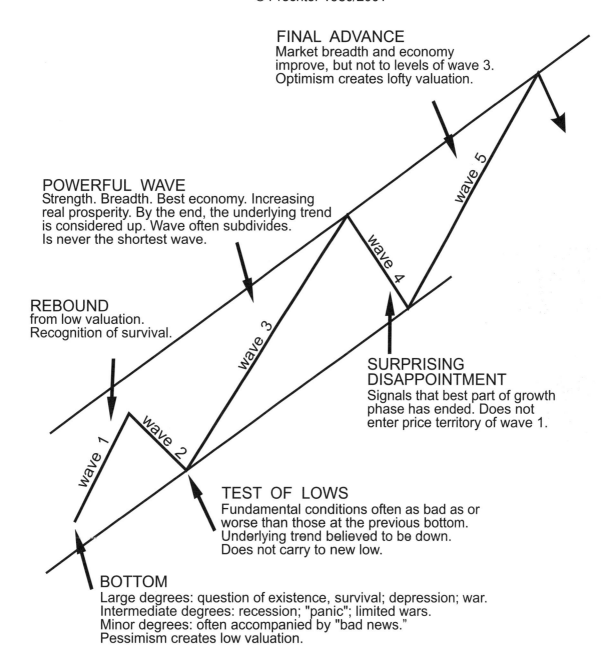

**FINAL ADVANCE**
Market breadth and economy
improve, but not to levels of wave 3.
Optimism creates lofty valuation.

**POWERFUL WAVE**
Strength. Breadth. Best economy. Increasing
real prosperity. By the end, the underlying trend
is considered up. Wave often subdivides.
Is never the shortest wave.

**REBOUND**
from low valuation.
Recognition of survival.

**SURPRISING
DISAPPOINTMENT**
Signals that best part of growth
phase has ended. Does not
enter price territory of wave 1.

**TEST OF LOWS**
Fundamental conditions often as bad as or
worse than those at the previous bottom.
Underlying trend believed to be down.
Does not carry to new low.

**BOTTOM**
Large degrees: question of existence, survival; depression; war.
Intermediate degrees: recession; "panic"; limited wars.
Minor degrees: often accompanied by "bad news."
Pessimism creates low valuation.

*Figure 3-1*

## Two Reliable Price Relationships

The fact that the Cycle-degree advance from 1974 is a fifth wave is important because there are several guidelines of wave development that indicate what the extent of a fifth wave is likely to be. Though Elliott described primarily the repeating *qualitative* aspects of financial markets' price structure, his few specific observations about quantities have stood the test of time. In the 1940s, he observed that there are two ways that fifth waves are typically related to preceding price action. He noted that when a third wave is extended, the first and fifth waves tend to be about the same size. He also noted two cases in which an extended fifth wave had a Fibonacci relationship to the entire distance covered by the first through third waves. On arithmetic scale, this relationship held true for the 1930s bull market and for the 1920s bull market up to the 1928 peak, as you can see by the circled notes in Figure 3-2, from his 1946 book, *Nature's Law* (republished in *R.N. Elliott's Masterworks*, 1980/1996).

With subsequent research, I was able to add some nuances to his formulas. As stated in Chapter 4 of *Elliott Wave Principle* (p.128), they are as follows:

> **When wave 3 is extended, waves 1 and 5 tend towards equality or a .618 relationship.**
>
> **Wave 5's length is sometimes related by the Fibonacci ratio to the length of wave 1 through wave 3.**

We can condense these expressions to say that in most cases,

> **wave 5**
>
> should have a Fibonacci relationship to
>
> **wave 1**, or
>
> **the net travel of waves 1 through 3** (henceforth labeled "1-3")
>
> or **both.**

Figures 3-3 and 3-4, from *Elliott Wave Principle*, show two illustrations of such relationships. Figure 3-5, also from that book, shows an idealized wave in which wave ⑤ satisfies both guidelines in being related by Fibonacci to wave ① and to waves ①-③. As we will see, the DJIA met this idealization at the January 2000 top.

## From R.N. Elliott's *Nature's Law* (1946)

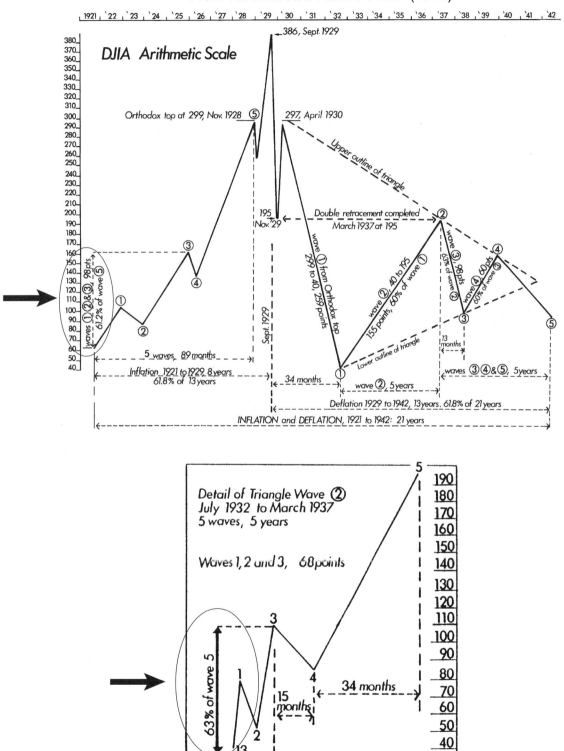

*Figure 3-2*

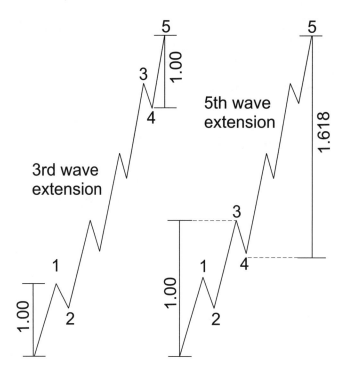

Figure 3-3                    Figure 3-4

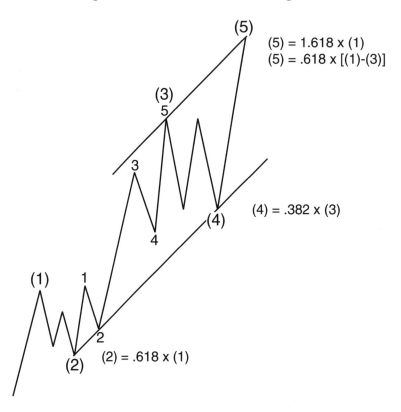

(5) = 1.618 x (1)
(5) = .618 x [(1)-(3)]

(4) = .382 x (3)

(2) = .618 x (1)

Figure 3-5

Fifth waves are the most important waves for target projection since they terminate larger advances, but, as *Elliott Wave Principle* explains, "Actually, *all three* motive waves tend to be related by Fibonacci mathematics, whether by equality, 1.618 or 2.618 (whose inverses are .618 and .382)." The components of Cycle wave V and Supercycle wave (V) bear out this observation. In our upcoming investigation, we will also discover that sometimes the relationships between other waves in the structure extend past $\phi^2$ to higher powers of phi.

## Previous Price Projections

Using the first guideline, Frost and I noted in 1978 that wave V should probably be expected to top out upon reaching equality with wave I, measured from the 1974 low. (That event occurred with striking precision at the 1987 high; see Figure 5-11.) In September 1982, I postulated that a higher "orthodox bottom" had occurred the previous month, which raised the projection to Dow 3885, later adjusted to 3664. (For the original commentary, see the Appendix to *Elliott Wave Principle*.) This target appeared absurdly high to financial professionals and the public, who were deeply cautious at the time. Yet a great bull market for wave V was nothing less than an imperative, so virtual certainty accompanied the exercise of forecasting at least a quintupling of the averages from 1982.

When the Dow exceeded 3664 in 1994, it was clear that wave V would have to satisfy another relationship to the Supercycle's earlier waves. Which one it would be proved elusive because given the knowledge available at that time, a Dow of nearly 12,000 would have been seen as far surpassing old norms. *The Elliott Wave Theorist* justified its pursuit of a target by noting from experience, "the market's long term patterns are always precise." Section Two of *View from the Top of the Grand Supercycle* recounts these attempts. They are worth reviewing if only to show that *the approach was consistent*, at least in this regard, and as we will see, it is these very relationships that the ultimate gain of wave V quite simply and elegantly satisfied.

## Previous Time Projections

As Cycle wave V progressed through the 1990s, I made three essential observations, involving both symmetry and Fibonacci, with respect to the *time element* of Cycle wave V and Supercycle wave (V). The first involved the symmetry in related waves (sometimes involving Fibonacci), as already shown in Figures 2-2 and 2-3. The second observation involved Fibonacci time relationships among the advancing Primary waves of Cycle wave V. The third involved the remarkable Fibonacci cross-relationships that appeared to exist between the sub-waves of Cycle wave V and those of Supercycle wave (V). You can see examples of these approaches in *View from the Top*, and all three of them are applied to the completed structure in forthcoming chapters.

## Resolution

*View from the Top* recounts EWT's forecast from April 1998 that the Dow would top when wave V reached a .618 relationship to waves I-III. I first applied it to the *1974* low, as shown in Figure 3-6. When the projected level of 8839 was exceeded, even our subscribers knew what the next level should be, which was derived by applying the same relationship to the other candidate for the end of wave IV, the *1982* low. In May 1998, we published that projection to 11,889, which turned out to be only 1.5% away from the high recorded in January 2000, as illustrated in Figure 3-7. As it turns out (see Figure C-1 in Appendix

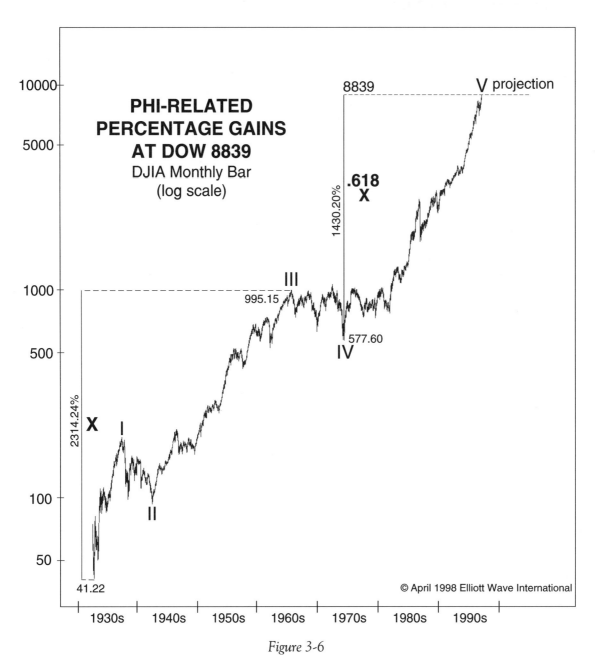

*Figure 3-6*

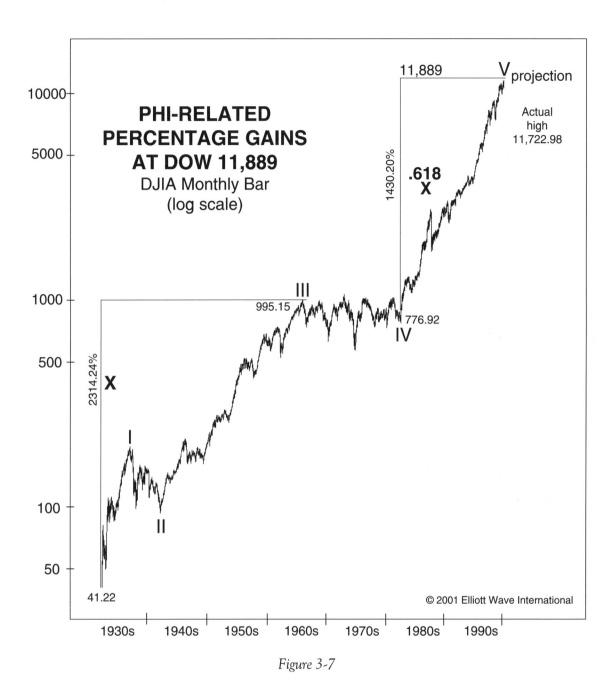

Figure 3-7

C), the percentage gain of wave V is .609 times that of waves I-III. This value is certainly close to .618, but as we will see, the ratio of their multiples are even more interesting.

As the DJIA crested in January 2000, other price and time relationships fell into place, which were reported in the February 2000 issue of *The Elliott Wave Theorist*. That entire report is available in *View from the Top*, but the price-related illustrations are reproduced here as Figures 3-8 and 3-9, which show that the Dow's price values at the January 2000 high are close to previous peak values multiplied by a power of φ.

As published in *The Elliott Wave Theorist* of February 2000

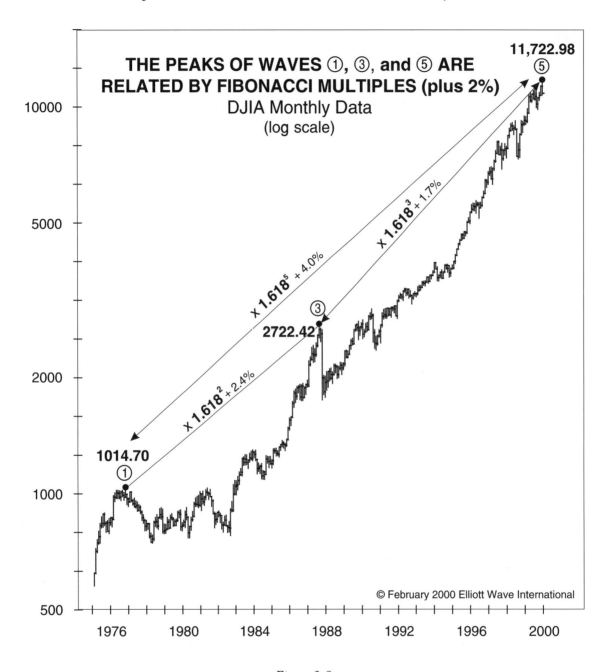

*Figure 3-8*

As published in *The Elliott Wave Theorist* of February 2000

*Figure 3-9*

*Chapter 4*

## *Preliminary Considerations for Price and Time Analysis*

### Wave Multiples Are Often Close to Fibonacci Fractions

Some of nature's forms, such as spiraling seashells, can reflect the irrational number phi, but most of them, such as flower, seed and stem arrangements in plants, use whole numbers to generate Fibonacci number *fractions*, which deviate from the phi limit ratio (.618). Upon investigating the numbers involved, I observe that the market's price and time relationships are usually off slightly from the limit ratio. The data in these studies thus suggest that the mass psychology behind the stock market, for whatever reason, similarly adheres to Fibonacci number fractions. For reference, Table 4-A displays decimal expressions of ratios using Fibonacci numbers up to 144.

An infinite number of adjacent Fibonacci numbers produce ratios within a tight range between .615 and .619. There are two major outliers from this cluster. One of them is equality (1/1) and the other is 1.5 (1/2). Closer to the realm of the limit ratio phi, there are three outliers: 2/3, 3/5 and 5/8. Two of their decimal expressions are above .618, and one is below it. Figure 4-1 displays these points. When checking waves for precise Fibonacci relationships, one apparently must investigate not just the area near .618 but also .600, .625 and .667.

## NUMERATOR

| | 1 | 2 | 3 | 5 | 8 | 13 | 21 | 34 | 55 | 89 | 144 |
|---|---|---|---|---|---|---|---|---|---|---|---|
| 1 | 1 | 2 | 3 | 5 | 8 | 13 | 21 | 34 | 55 | 89 | 144 |
| 2 | 0.5 | 1 | 1.5 | 2.5 | 4 | 6.5 | 10.5 | 17 | 27.5 | 44.5 | 72 |
| 3 | 0.333 | 0.667 | 1 | 1.67 | 2.667 | 4.333 | 7 | 11.33 | 18.33 | 29.67 | 48 |
| 5 | 0.2 | 0.4 | 0.6 | 1 | 1.6 | 2.6 | 4.2 | 6.8 | 11 | 17.8 | 28.8 |
| 8 | 0.125 | 0.25 | 0.375 | 0.625 | 1 | 1.625 | 2.625 | 4.25 | 6.875 | 11.13 | 18 |
| 13 | 0.077 | 0.154 | 0.231 | 0.385 | 0.615 | 1 | 1.615 | 2.615 | 4.231 | 6.846 | 11.08 |
| 21 | 0.048 | 0.095 | 0.143 | 0.238 | 0.381 | 0.619 | 1 | 1.619 | 2.619 | 4.238 | 6.857 |
| 34 | 0.029 | 0.059 | 0.088 | 0.147 | 0.235 | 0.382 | 0.618 | 1 | 1.618 | 2.618 | 4.235 |
| 55 | 0.018 | 0.036 | 0.055 | 0.091 | 0.146 | 0.236 | 0.382 | 0.618 | 1 | 1.618 | 2.618 |
| 89 | 0.011 | 0.022 | 0.034 | 0.056 | 0.090 | 0.146 | 0.236 | 0.382 | 0.618 | 1 | 1.618 |
| 144 | 0.007 | 0.014 | 0.021 | 0.035 | 0.055 | 0.090 | 0.146 | 0.236 | 0.382 | 0.618 | 1 |

**DENOMINATOR** (vertical axis label)

Toward
Perfect
Ratios

*Table 4-A*

Fibonacci numbers are not the only numbers that produce a Fibonacci relation-ship. A denominator can be chosen for any whole-number numerator so that the ratio is closest to phi. Continuing the process with the numerator as a new denominator creates a new "Fibonacci" whole number progression in which the limit ratio approaches phi. For example, 7/11 is .63636, 11/18 is .61111, 18/29 is .62069, and so on. The most interesting property of all sequences derived from such exercises (such as the Lucas sequence: 1, 3, 4, 7, 11, 18, etc.) is their ratio progression, which approaches .618 regardless of which two numbers begin the additive sequence. Tables 4-B through 4-D show an array of Fibonacci whole-number fractions for quick reference. The first table expresses $\phi$, the second $\phi^2$ and the third $\phi^3$. Fibonacci number ratios are shown in bold print. These expressions go to five decimal places, though two or three are sufficient for everyday application to waves of Primary and lesser degree. Using every whole number as a numerator, we find that 4/7 (.57143), is the only additional whole number ratio that lies outside the range of .60 to .67.

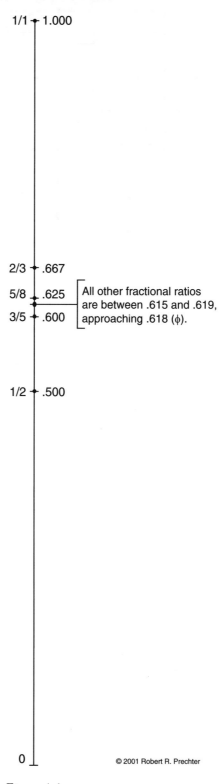

*Figure 4-1*

**DECIMAL EXPRESSIONS OF WHOLE-NUMBER FIBONACCI FRACTIONS AND THEIR INVERSES, APPROACHING $\phi$ (.618/1.618)**

| RATIO | $1/1$ | $1/2$ | $2/3$ | $3/5$ | $4/7$ | $5/8$ | $7/11$ | $8/13$ |
|---|---|---|---|---|---|---|---|---|
| DECIMAL | 1.00 | .50 | .66667 | .6 | .57143 | .625 | .63636 | .61538 |
| INVERSE | 1.00 | 2.00 | 1.5 | 1.6667 | 1.75 | 1.6 | 1.57143 | 1.625 |
| | $9/14$ | $11/18$ | $12/19$ | $13/21$ | $17/28$ | $18/29$ | $19/31$ | $21/34$ |
| | .64286 | .61111 | .63158 | .61905 | .60714 | .62069 | .61290 | .61765 |
| | 1.5555 | 1.63636 | 1.58333 | 1.61538 | 1.64706 | 1.61111 | 1.63157 | 1.61905 |

*Table 4-B*

**DECIMAL EXPRESSIONS OF ALTERNATE WHOLE-NUMBER FIBONACCI FRACTIONS AND THEIR INVERSES, APPROACHING $\phi^2$(.382/2.618)**

| RATIO | $1/3$ | $2/5$ | $3/8$ | $4/11$ | $5/13$ |
|---|---|---|---|---|---|
| DECIMAL | .33333 | .4 | .375 | .36364 | .38462 |
| INVERSE | 3.00 | 2.5 | 2.6667 | 2.75 | 2.6 |
| | $7/18$ | $8/21$ | $9/23$ | $11/29$ | $13/34$ |
| | .38889 | .38095 | .39130 | .37931 | .38235 |
| | 2.57143 | 2.625 | 2.55556 | 2.63636 | 2.61538 |

*Table 4-C*

**DECIMAL EXPRESSIONS OF SECOND ALTERNATE WHOLE-NUMBER FIBONACCI FRACTIONS AND THEIR INVERSES, APPROACHING $\phi^3$(.236/4.236)**

| RATIO | $1/5$ | $2/8$ | $3/13$ | $4/17$ | $5/21$ |
|---|---|---|---|---|---|
| DECIMAL | .2 | .25 | .23077 | .23529 | .23810 |
| INVERSE | 5 | 4 | 4.33333 | 4.25 | 4.2 |
| | $6/25$ | $7/30$ | $8/34$ | $9/38$ | $11/47$ | $13/55$ |
| | .24 | .23333 | .23529 | .23684 | .23404 | .23636 |
| | 4.16667 | 4.28571 | 4.25 | 4.2222 | 4.27273 | 4.23076 |

*Table 4-D*

Let's apply this new perspective involving decimals and Fibonacci ratios to Figures 3-8 and 3-9, the observations made immediately following the Dow's January 2000 peak. Figures 4-2 and 4-3 show the same relationships in terms of multiples related by powers of phi but with the "leeway" expressed not as percentage differences from powers of the limit ratio but rather as differences in the value for the nearest whole-number Fibonacci fractions. This exercise reveals information that we did not see before. For example, five out of the six multiples derive from a phi value of approximately 1.63 (inverse .613). This consistency, among six multiples pertaining to five turning points decades apart, is quite striking. The fractions nearest these decimal expressions are 13/8, 21/13, 18/11 and 31/19.

For practical application, we must determine what is an acceptable approximation of a Fibonacci ratio. When dealing with near term movements in the market, a target calculation using .60-.67 produces so small a range that the practical differences within the range are negligible. For waves within a 20 percent move in the Dow, for example, the resulting target range is less than 1 percent of the value of the index. However, when dealing with a Supercycle lasting seven decades and covering a gain of over 20,000 percent, the difference between the high and low of the range is of practical significance. In the case of the phi relationship for wave V that we will see in Figure 5-1, the .60-to-.67 range (from 11,254.03 to 12,505.10) covers about 1200 points, or 10 percent, of the value of the index. Because the range of .60-.67 produces a substantial leeway, it is not an acceptable targeting standard when dealing with long term waves.

There is another reason to demand a narrower range. When dealing with powers of $\phi$, a 10 percent range of acceptability for the root widens so rapidly when brought to powers that any number will produce a Fibonacci root at some power above the fourth, which negates any value in finding it. (The spreads go as follows: .60-.67, .36-.4445, .216-.2963, .1296-.1976, .0778-.1317, at which point the ranges overlap.) Our culprits in the large range cited above are clearly the moderate outliers, 2/3 (.67) and 3/5 (.60). The next most outlying fraction, 5/8 (.625), produces a significantly lesser deviation from the limit ratio of only .007.

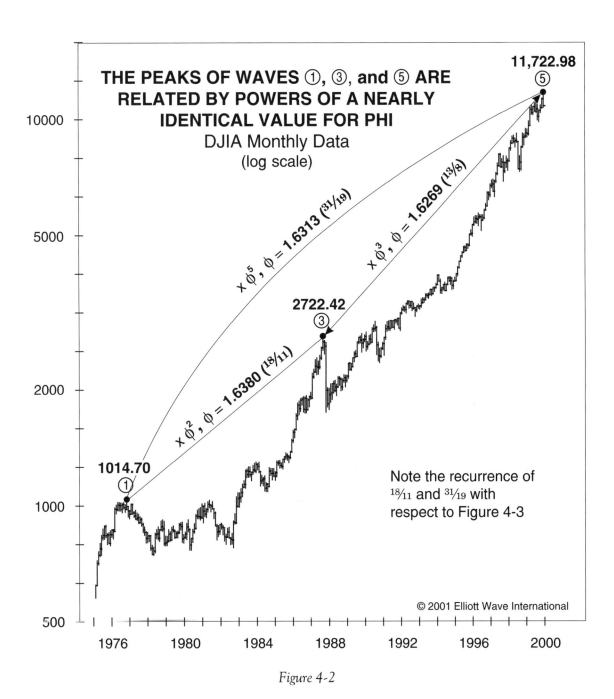

Figure 4-2

*Figure 4-3*

## Identifying Phi

Upon reviewing the decimal and fractional expressions presented in Chapters 5 through 11, I find that the majority of them are extremely close to expressing powers of Fibonacci number fractions, primarily 2/3, 3/5, 5/8 and 8/13. Eighty percent of the decimal expressions for $\phi$ are within .0033 (0.5 percent) of the 2/3 fraction, .0010 (0.17 percent) of the 3/5 fraction and .00136 (0.22 percent) of any other fraction using adjacent Fibonacci numbers. The spread for the 3/5 fraction is small because there is only one example that isn't either perfect or an outlier. To create a reasonable range that will serve future investigations and provide a basis for generalized probability studies, Table 4-E widens the allowed spread from .0010 to .0017 (0.28 percent). The first six ranges are thus as follows:

| | Fraction | Spread | Range |
|---|---|---|---|
| | 2/3 | .6667 ± .0033 | .6634 - .6700 |
| | 3/5 | .6000 ± .0017 | .5983 - .6017 |
| *Table 4-E* | 5/8 | .6250 ± .0015 | .6235 - .6265 |
| | 8/13 | .615385 ± .001354 | .6140 - .61674 |
| | 13/21 | .61905 ± .00136 | .6177 - .6204 |
| | 21/34 | .61765 ± .00136 | .6163 - .6190 |

The final three ranges overlap, and all successive Fibonacci ratios fall within that range, so we are left with only four distinct ranges for Fibonacci fractions:

| | Fraction | Spread | Leeway | Range |
|---|---|---|---|---|
| | 2/3 | **.6667** ± .0033 | 0.5% | **.6634 - .6700** |
| *Table 4-F* | 3/5 | **.6000** ± .0017 | 0.28% | **.5983 - .6017** |
| | 5/8 | **.6250** ± .0015 | 0.24% | **.6235 - .6265** |
| All other Fib# ratios | **.6172** ± .0032 | 0.5% | **.6140 - .6204** |

The final category is interesting because it reveals that all other Fibonacci number ratios, when each has a leeway of 0.22 percent, fall within a range that is only ½ percent of the center number, the same leeway given to the 2/3 fraction. The sum total of these four ranges is .0194, which is about 3.1 percent of .62.

Table 4-F is the only table you need for assessing the relationships shown in this book. The same ratios and ranges may be found *inverted, subtracted from 1 or raised to a power*, but they all derive from this table. For explanatory purposes, we will now examine some of those equivalent expressions.

Inverses are equal expressions of fractional relationships. If we have 5 of one thing and 8 of another, we can express the relationship as 5/8 or 8/5. So, for example, in terms of expressing a relationship between two values, the decimal 1.6129 is *the same as* .62. Like-wise, 1.5 is the same as .6667, 1.6667 is the same as .60, and so on. Table 4-G presents a list of the same numbers as those in the table above but expressed in decimal inverses:

| Inverse | Spread | Range |
|---|---|---|
| 3/2 | **1.5000** ± .0075 | **1.4925 – 1.5074** |
| 5/3 | **1.6667** ± .0050 | **1.6620 – 1.6714** |
| 8/5 | **1.6000** ± .0038 | **1.5962 – 1.6038** |
| all other Fib# ratios | **1.62026** ± .0084 | **1.61186 – 1.62866** |

*Table 4-G*

In many cases, expressions labeled $\phi^2$ in this book are just alternate expressions of $\phi$ because they represent the other side of a golden section, as depicted on in Figure 0-2. That is, they are 1-$\phi$. For example, 1/3 is 1-2/3, 2/5 is 1-3/5, 3/8 is 1-5/8, and so on. Figure 11-2 provides an example of how the decimals .3736 and .6264 actually express the same fact regarding the subdivision of a line. Other examples of $\phi^2$ ratios that may be expressed as 1-$\phi$ include those in Figures 7-1, 8-1, 9-1 and most of the illustrations in Chapters 10 and 11. In these cases, Table 4-F expresses their boundaries of acceptability. Of course, when applying the spreads in Table 4-F to each 1-$\phi$ value, which is smaller than its corresponding $\phi$ value, the leeway expands, as shown in Table 4-H.

| Fraction | Spread | Leeway | Range |
|---|---|---|---|
| 1/3 (1-2/3) | **.3333** ± .0033 | 0.99% | **.3300 - .3366** |
| 2/5 (1-3/5) | **.4000** ± .0017 | 0.43% | **.3983 - .4017** |
| 3/8 (1-5/8) | **.3750** ± .0015 | 0.40% | **.3735 - .3765** |
| all other Fib# ratios | **.3288** ± .0032 | 0.97% | **.3256 - .3320** |

*Table 4-H*

As it happens, the 1-$\phi$ relationships identified in these studies fall much closer to precise fractional and limit ratio expressions than such leeways allow. For example, the two 1/3 ratios listed are within .0016 of the ideal decimal and thus require less than half of the expanded leeway afforded the expression, 1-2/3. The ensuing illustrations (except for one marked with a †) actually display fractions between alternate Fibonacci numbers to within the percents indicated in Table I, which are much smaller than those in Table 4-H:

| Fractions Found | Spread Utilized | Leeway Utilized | Range Utilized |
|---|---|---|---|
| 1/3 (1-2/3) | .3333 ± .0017 | 0.5% | .3316 - .3350 |
| 2/5 (1-3/5) | .4000 ± 0 | 0.0% | .4000 - .4000 |
| 3/8 (1-5/8) | .3750 ± .0015 | 0.40% | .3735 - .3765 |
| each subsequent Fib# ratio | | 0.25% | |

*Table 4-I*

All fractions found that involve alternate Fibonacci numbers from 5/13 onward fall within the range for "all other Fib# ratios$^2$" shown in Table 4-J.

## Identifying $\phi^2$

Multiplicative expressions of $\phi^2$ do appear in this book (see for example Figure 5-8). As the numbers in the fractions rise, the decimal expressions converge toward the limit ratio .382. Here is a table for quick reference of $\phi^2$ fractional values. Given the ranges for $\phi$ in Table 4-F, the leeway and allowable range for each $\phi^2$ value expand to the following:

| | Fraction | Spread | Leeway | Range |
|---|---|---|---|---|
| | $(2/3)^2$ | **.4445** ± .0044 | 0.99% | **.4401 - .4489** |
| | $(3/5)^2$ | **.3600** ± .0022 | 0.56% | **.3580 - .3620** |
| | $(5/8)^2$ | **.3906** ± .0019 | 0.49% | **.3888 - .3925** |
| all other (Fib# ratios)$^2$ | | **.3809** ± .0040 | 1.05% | **.3770 - .3849** |

*Table 4-J*

The sum total of the four ranges in Table J is .0249, which is about 6.6 percent of .38.

All ratios expressed in upcoming illustrations adhere to the narrow limits expressed in the preceding tables unless noted by the symbol †. As you encounter decimal expressions of Fibonacci ratios, refer back to the bold ranges in Tables 4-F through 4-J to become oriented to their allowed ranges. (Keep in mind, though, that the only table actually required for this book is Table 4-F, along with the perspective provided in Table 4-I.)

## On Probabilities

The studies in Chapters 5 through 11 utilize a specific list of eleven Elliott waves that took place between 1932 and 2000: the Primary degree waves within wave V, the Cycle degree waves within wave (V), and wave (V) itself. Some of the price studies use the net distance of waves one through three at Primary or at Cycle degree, for a total of 13 structures. Here is the list: ①, ②, ③, ④, ⑤, ①-③, I, II, III, IV, V, I-III and (V). (There are also references to the net of waves one through four and of waves four through five, but these sections may be considered derivatives of waves five and one through three, respectively.) If we find a large number of relationships among waves in this predetermined list as either Fibonacci number fractions or as decimals within our allowable ranges for $\phi$ and $\phi^2$, we can conclude that few of them are there by chance.

Given the ranges expressed in Table 4-F, we can do some calculations that speak to the probabilities of finding a phi root at each power by chance. At each power, the spread as a percentage of the center number expands. For example, at the 2nd power, instead of 0.5, 0.3 and 0.22 percent for 2/3, 3/5 and all other Fibonacci number ratios, the spreads are 1.0, 0.6 and 0.44 percent for $(2/3)^2$, $(3/5)^2$ and all other Fibonacci number ratios squared.

At successively higher powers, the spreads continue to widen, although by decreasing multiples.

Because the total value of the three ranges listed in Table 4-F is .0194, the spread is ± .0097 around a representative number. Around the ratio .62, the spreads through the 16th power are as follows: (1st).6103-.6297, (2nd).37247-.39652, (3rd).22732-.24969, (4th).13873-.15723, (5th).08467-.09901, (6th).05167-.06235, (7th).03154-.03926, (8th).01925-.02472, (9th).011746-.015567, (10th).007169-.009803. (11th).00437-.00617, (12th).00267-.00389, (13th).00163-.00245, (14th).000995-.001541, (15th).000607-.000971, (16th).0003704-.000611. (These are not the ranges used but are merely for the purposes of addressing probabilities.) Taking each range as a percentage of itself plus the open range above it, we have the following probabilities that any decimal between 0 and 1 will have a Fibonacci root:

1st power: .0194/.3897 = 4.98% (1 in 20)
2nd power: .02405/.23783 = 10.11% (1 in 10)
3rd power: .02237/.14515 = 15.41% (1 in 6.5)
4th power: .01850/.08859 = 20.88% (1 in 5)
5th power: .01434/.05406 = 26.53% (1 in 4)
6th power: .01068/.03300 = 32.36% (1 in 3)

9th power: .00382/.00750 = 50.9% (1 in 2)
16th power: 100% (1 in 1).

The above odds would speak directly to the probability for each of the decimals and ratios displayed in these studies *if* the full range of tolerance were required in every instance. To figure the true probabilities, we would have to calculate them for the precision of each number. Most of the numbers are not near the maximum leeway for each fraction. In fact, many of them are either precise or off by less than 1/10 of one percent, an extremely small amount, particularly given that most of the expressions in this book are to the first or second power. Therefore, the *actual* differences from perfect ratios are much smaller than the above-listed spreads. For example, Figure 5-1 will show a ratio of two multiples, each to four decimal places, that is 5/8, or .625, to the first power. Carrying the multiples out to eight decimal places gives an answer of .625001648. Within an available range of .3897, the probability of any ratio between adjacent Fibonacci numbers (from 2/3 on up) appearing to that degree of precision is .000001648/.3897, or .000004229, which is .0004229%, or about 1 in 236,000. Dividing that number by the number of first-degree Fibonacci number ratios expressed in these studies, which is six (2/3, 3/5, 5/8, 8/13,13/34 and the limit ratio .618), gives less than 1 in 39,000 odds of finding by chance any one among them to that degree of precision.

Figure 5-13 provides another instructive example of the true probabilities. One of its expressions is $(8/13)^6$. The list above suggests that the odds of its appearance are 1 in 3. In fact, to seven decimal places, the value is .6153635, which is only .0000211 away from the decimal value of 8/13, which is .6153846. With an available range of .03300, the probability of any ratio between adjacent Fibonacci numbers (from 2/3 on up) appearing at the sixth power to that degree of precision is .0000211/.033, or .0006394, which is .06394%, or 1 in 1564. Dividing that number by the six Fibonacci-number fractional roots allowed in these studies (only two actually appear to the 6th power) gives about 1 in 260 chance of finding any one among them to that degree of precision at the sixth power. These odds are quite different from 1 in 3.

Eighty-one percent of the relationships described in Chapters 5 through 11 are to only the first or second power, which means that they have a particularly low probability of having appeared by chance. Table 4-K lists the total number of ratios displayed at each power. Repeated expressions of a particular relationship are counted only once. Different ratios expressing the same general idea are counted separately. In this summary, ratios between adjacent numbers in a whole-number additive sequence whose limit ratio is phi are designated as being $\phi$ to the first power, as are ratios between alternate numbers, which are simply 1-$\phi$. Ratios between adjacent Fibonacci numbers that are squared, cubed and so on are designated $\phi^2$, $\phi^3$, etc. in Table 4-K.

| | Number of Relationships Displayed at Each Power in Chapters 5 through 11 | |
|---|---|---|
| | 1st power ($\phi$ and 1-$\phi$): | 60 |
| | 2nd power ($\phi^2$): | 11 |
| *Table 4-K* | 3rd power ($\phi^3$): | 5 |
| | 4th power ($\phi^4$): | 5 |
| | 5th power ($\phi^5$): | 2 |
| | 6th power ($\phi^6$): | 3 |
| | 7th power ($\phi^7$): | 1 |
| | 8th power ($\phi^8$): | 1 |

To obtain the probability of finding all the Fibonacci ratio relationships in the body of this book would require finalizing rules for determining in advance which wave relationships would be investigated and then *multiplying all of the probabilities together*. Four types of relationships that I investigated were in fact determined in advance from prior rules or research, specifically, waves ① vs. ⑤, ①-③ vs. ⑤, ① vs. ③ and ② vs. ④. Most of the other relationships "make sense" from the standpoint of wave structure, for example, cross-relating the same wave numbers, such as ①/I, ②/II, ③/III, ④/IV and ⑤/V. Multiplying all the outcomes displayed in Chapters 5 through 11 together would probably push the overall odds of finding all these expressions at least to one in millions. Perhaps a statistician would have further insight regarding this topic.

In all, there are 88 Fibonacci fractions expressed in the charts in Chapters 5 through 11, as listed in Table 4-L. Of them, 76, or 86.4 percent, fall within the ranges specified in Tables 4-F, 4-H and 4-J. Among the 12 that do not, eight are very close to "Fibonacci" fractions using non-Fibonacci numbers. Among them, three are between 0.08 and 0.13 percent from 11/18, two are 0.22 and 0.44 percent from 17/28, two are 0.05 and 0.10 percent from 19/31 and one is 0.24 percent from 18/29. We may consider these acceptable ratios, but doing do would require re-stating the probabilities for finding such ratios by incorporating ranges for all ratios listed in Table 4-B and thus expanding our total range value. Among the final four fractions, two are 0.60 percent from 3/5, one is 0.78 percent from 5/3, and one is 2.0 percent from 2/3. Also included in Table 4-L and later illustrations are some precise 1/2 and 1/1 time ratios, as well as a decimal that is 0.06 percent from .50 (1/2) and a decimal that is 0.43 percent from 1.00 (1/1), which I deem to be within an acceptable range for each of those fractions.

## Price Multiples

Comparing major waves' components in arithmetic terms (the number of "points") is often meaningless; they must be stated as multiples or percentages in order to express their relative achievements. A doubling of prices can be called a multiple of 2 or as having an end value equal to 200 percent of its starting value. We can also express the extent as a *gain* of 100 percent. For substantial moves, numbers expressing *multiples* are nearly the same as those expressing percentage gains. A 900 percent gain, for example, is a multiple of 10; a 1900 percent gain is a multiple of 20, and so on. The difference is always 100 percent, or a multiple of 1.

As it turns out, the ratios between measurements for movements in the Supercycle and its components are far closer to perfection when relating them in terms of their multiples rather than their percentage gains. Most of the diagrams and calculations in the studies involving price refer to wave extents as multiples of their starting points. (In the illustrations, "m" stands for "multiple.") The ranges for corrections are expressed as multiples from low to high, not high to low, which keeps the measurements of wave extents consistent. Decimals are matched to the closest whole-number Fibonacci ratios where applicable. I hesitate to presume that the Dow is always searching for such specific ratios, though repeatedly the most important wave relationships are exact Fibonacci fractions or nearly so. The price multiples that waves achieve are repeatedly related to each other by expressions of phi, carried to a power.

I have no answer to the question of why a few sets of waves relate by Fibonacci arithmetically (see Figure 3-2) or in terms of percentages (see Appendix C) rather than

**TABLE 4-L: LIST OF VALUES SHOWN IN THE ILLUSTRATIONS IN CHAPTERS 5-11**

Numbers in parentheses are the fractions that the preceding decimals approach.

Numbers in bold denote percentages away from perfect Fibonacci number fractions. (.09 means 0.09 percent, not 9 percent.)

Italic numbers to the right in each box indicate the power of the phi root. 1-φ expressions within tolerance for φ are marked to the first power.

The symbol † indicates ratios outside the narrow limits listed in Tables 4-F, 4-G and 4-J.

| Figure | Values | Power |
|---|---|---|
| Figure 5-1 | 0.625 (5/8) **0** | 1 |
| Figure 5-2 | repeat | |
| Figure 5-3 | 1.6266 (13/8) **.09** | 3 |
| Figure 5-4 | repeats | |
| Figure 5-5 | repeats | |
| Figure 5-6 | 1.6377† (18/11) **.08** | 5 |
| Figure 5-7 | 1.5015 (3/2) **.10** | 2 |
| | 0.6636 (2/3) **.47** | 2 |
| | 0.6634 (2/3) **.49** | 2 |
| | 0.6196 (13/21) **.08** | 1 |
| Figure 5-8 | 1.5042 (3/2) **.28** | 4 |
| | 3 repeats | |
| Figure 5-9 | 0.6131† (19/31) **.05** [(8/13) **.36**] | 5 |
| | 0.6044† (17/28) **.44** | 2 |
| Figure 5-10 | one repeat | |
| | 0.6123† (19/31) **.10** [(8/13) **.50**] | 1 |
| | 0.6130 (19/31) **.02** [(8/13) **.39**] [(3/8)$^3$ **.21**] [(3/13)$^2$ **.22**] | 6 |
| Figure 5-11 | 1.6201 (34/21) **.06** | 4 |
| | 1.0006 (1/1) **.06** | 1 |
| | 1.6269 (13/8) **.12** | 3 |
| | 1.6269 (13/8) **.12** | 3 |
| Figure 5-12 | repeats | |
| Figure 5-13 | .59904 (3/5) **.16** | 8 |
| | .62597 (5/8) **.16** | 7 |
| | .61536 (8/13) **0** | 6 |
| Figure 6-1 | 1.6189 (φ) **.06** | 1 |
| Figure 6-2 | 1.6009 (8/5) **.06** | 1 |
| Figure 6-3 | repeats | |
| Figure 6-4 | repeats | |
| Figure 6-5 | repeats | |
| Figure 6-6 | repeats | |
| Figure 6-7 | 1.6379† (18/11) **.09** | 2 |
| | 1.6797† (5/3) **.78** | 2 |
| | 1.6435† (28/17) **.22** | 2 |
| | [avg not counted] | |
| Figure 6-8 | repeats | |
| Figure 6-9 | repeats | |
| Figure 6-10 | repeats | |
| Figure 6-11 | repeats | |
| Figure 6-12 | repeat | |
| | 1.4993 (3/2) **.05** | 1 |
| Figure 6-13 | 1.5327/1.5292† (3/2) **2.0** [(14/9) **1.6**] (counts once) | 1 |
| Figure 6-14 | 1.0043 (1/1) **.43** | 1 |
| Figure 6-15 | 1.628 (13/8) **.18** | 3 |
| Figure 7-1 | 0.3725† (11/18)$^2$ **.13** [(3/8) **.67**] | 1 |
| | 0.3349 (1/3) **.48** | 1 |
| | 0.3322 (1/3) **.33** | 1 |
| Figure 7-2 | 0.6681 (2/3) **.21** | 1 |
| | 0.6246 (5/8) **.06** | 1 |
| Figure 7-3 | repeats | |
| Figure 7-4 | 0.6647 (2/3) **.30** | 4 |
| | 0.6154 (8/13) **0** | 6 |
| | 0.0543 (3/55) **.37** [not counted] | |
| Figure 8-1 | 1/1 **0** 1/1 **0** 1/1 **0** 1/1 **0** 1/1 **0** | 11111 |
| | 1/2 **0** | 1 |
| | 13/34 **0** | 1 |
| Figure 9-1 | 2/5 **0** 5/13 **0** 2/13 **0** | 114 |
| Figure 9-2 | 0.3904 (5/8)$^2$ **.03** | 2 |
| | 0.3908 (5/8)$^2$ **.03** | 2 |
| | 0.6250 (5/8) **0** | 4 |
| Figure 9-3 | (1/1) **.32** | 1 |
| Figure 10-1 | 5/2 **0** 5/2 **0** 3/8 **0** 3/8 **0** 5/13 **0** | 11111 |
| | 8/21 **0** 13/34 **0** 13/34 **0** 13/34 **0** | 1111 |
| Figure 10-2 | 0.3810 (8/21) **.01** | 1 |
| | 0.3826 (13/34) **.05** | 1 |
| | 0.3821 (φ$^2$) **.03** | 1 |
| Figure 10-3 | 0.3845 (5/13) **.03** | 1 |
| | repeat | |
| | 0.3751 (3/8) **.03** | 1 |
| | 0.5003 (1/2) **.06** | 1 |
| Figure 10-4 | 0.3765 (3/8) **.40** [(19/31)$^2$ **.11**] [(8/13)$^2$ **.29**] | 1 |
| | 0.3827 (13/34) **.08** | 1 |
| Figure 10-5 | 0.3786 (11/29) **.18** [(8/13)$^2$ **.08**] | 2 |
| | 0.3837 (5/13) **.23** [(13/21)$^2$ **.05**] | 1 |
| | 0.3765 (3/8) **.40** [(19/31)$^2$ **.11**] [8/13)$^2$ **.29**] | 1 |
| | 0.3800 (8/21) **.25** | 1 |
| Figure 10-6 | one repeat | |
| | 0.3770 (19/31)$^2$ **.18** [(8/13)$^2$ **.22**] | 2 |
| Figure 10-7 | n/a | |
| Figure 10-8 | 0.3744 (3/8) **.16** | 1 |
| | 0.3762 (3/8) **.32** [(8/13)$^2$ **.31**] [(19/31)$^2$ **.08**] | 1 |
| | 0.3803 (8/21) **.18** [(21/34) **.16**] | 1 |
| | 0.3778 (11/29) **.40** [(8/13)$^2$ **.11**] | 2 |
| Figure 10-9 | repeats | |
| Figure 11-1 | 5/13 **0** 13/34 **0** 5/34 **0** | 111 |
| Figure 11-2 | 0.6264 (5/8) **.22** | 1 |
| | 0.3736 (3/8) **.43** [(11/18)$^2$ **.02**] | 1 |
| | 0.5964† (3/5) **.60** | 1 |
| | 0.6264 (5/8) **.22** | 1 |
| | 0.3736 (3/8) **.43** [(11/18)$^2$ **.02**] | 1 |
| | 0.5964† (3/5) **.60** | 1 |
| Figure 11-3 | essentially a repeat | |
| Figure 11-4 | repeats | |
| Figure 11-5 | repeats | |
| Figure 11-6 | repeats | |
| Figure 11-7 | repeats | |
| Figure 11-8 | 0.6154 (8/13) **0** | 1 |
| | 0.6222† (18/29) **.24** [(5/8) **.45**] | 1 |
| | [avg not counted] | |
| Figure 11-9 | 0.6179 (φ) **.02** | 1 |
| | 0.6197 (13/21) **.10** | 1 |
| Figure 11-10 | repeats | |
| Figure 11-11 | repeats | |
| Figure 11-12 | repeats | |
| Figure 11-13 | repeats | |

**TOTAL RATIOS: 88 (76 + 12†)**

Table 4-L

multiples. Understand that the first two types of ratios will be nearly identical in small waves and the second two will be nearly identical in large ones, mitigating their differences and further implying that arithmetic expressions may be irrelevant, leaving only percentages and multiples as reasonable bases for comparison. The evidence in this book seems to indicate that multiples are by far the market's preferred basis for Fibonacci expression.

Keep in mind that when you see decimals above 1.00, they are simply inverses of lesser ratios; for example, 1.50 is the inverse of .67, and 1.67 is the inverse of .60. I could have expressed every phi value as a decimal less than 1, but I preferred to maintain the values for wave I and waves I-III as the standards by which all other multiples are compared. This approach respects their practical utility as measuring units for predicting later termination points for wave five. When the related multiple is larger than one of these standards, then their relationship is expressed as the higher fraction.

If you decide to apply your calculator to compute the inverses of some of these decimals, realize that in rounding to four decimal places, sometimes the inverse of the displayed decimal can be slightly different from the decimal expression of the inverse ratio of the wave multiples, by .0001 or so. For best precision, calculate inverses using the wave multiples, which are provided in the graphs.

## Various Interpretations within Wave V

Contrary to the norm, several waves in these studies have multiple turning points. Wave V has two acceptable starting points: 1974 and 1982, each of which was recognized as such *at the time*. Commentary from 1982 in the Appendix of *Elliott Wave Principle* elaborates on this point, and *The Elliott Wave Theorist* referred continually to this duality. The price and time ratios described in this book show that the stock market has utilized them both in forming its Fibonacci relationships. (Appendix B explores a third starting point.)

There has also been an unusual choice of dates, and therefore prices, for marking the turns of Primary waves *within* Cycle wave V. For example, the S&P Composite index began wave V on 10/4/74, while the Dow's low occurred two months later, on 12/6/74. A wave pattern's termination point is called its "orthodox" end when that point differs from its price extreme. The price high of wave ① occurred on 9/21/76, while the orthodox top (based on wave structure; see Chapter 4 of *Elliott Wave Principle*) occurred three months later, on 12/31/76. Wave ② ended on 2/28/78 in the S&P and 3/27/80 in the Dow, but if wave IV is labeled at that low (per Appendix B), then wave ② would be labeled on 8/12/82. Wave ③ ended either at an orthodox top on 4/6/87 or at its price high on 8/25/87. Wave ④ bottomed on 10/19/87, but it is acceptable to mark the orthodox low on 12/4/87, 10/11/90 or 1/14/91. See Figures 4-4 through 4-7 for illustrations of these options. These latter two dates not only fit acceptable wave patterns in the Dow but they also make sense in terms of related events. In October 1990, for example, the Value Line Index and the

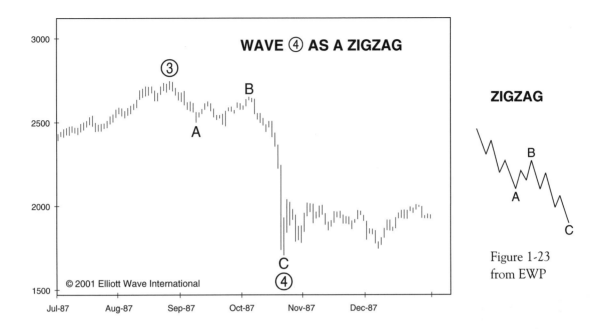

Figure 4-4

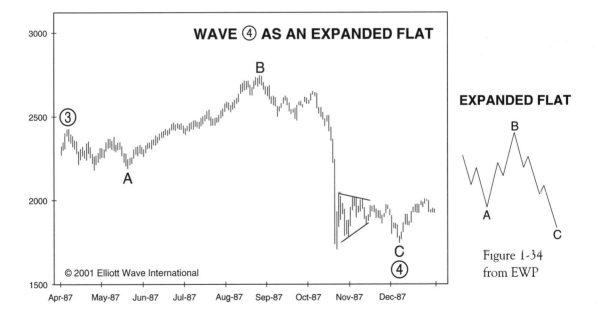

Figure 4-5

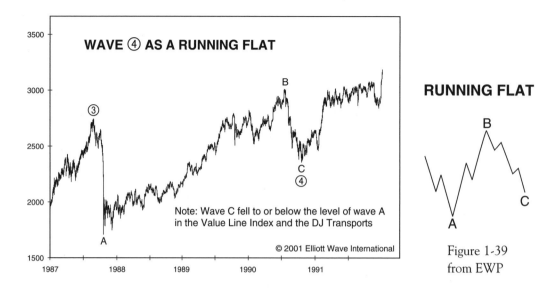

*Figure 4-6*

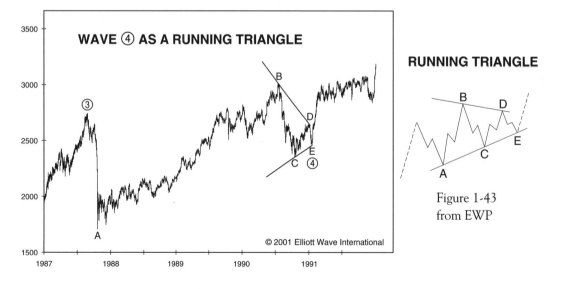

*Figure 4-7*

*Figure 4-8*

Dow Jones Transports approached and exceeded, respectively, their lows of 1987. (For a picture of this event, see Figure 12 on page 178 of *View From the Top of the Grand Supercycle* or Figure 16-3 or 19-3 in *The Wave Principle of Human Social Behavior*.) In other words, the Elliott wave interpretation shown in Figure 4-6 says something important about the market. At the January 1991 date illustrated in Figure 4-7, the U.S. dollar bottomed on the currency exchanges and the United States entered the Gulf War. Such events typically occur at the end of a corrective process. It is perhaps important to mention that *The Elliott Wave Theorist* recognized all of these alternatives in print, before any of the relationships presented here were known. In other words, that these various points are available for measurement is not the product of data fitting for the purposes of finding Fibonacci ratios. Rather, ratios are sought within variations of waves previously identified.

Wave ⑤ ended on two dates as well, on 1/14/00 in the Dow and on 3/24/00 in the S&P. Finally, as you can see in Figure 4-8, a close-up of the S&P's price action in 2000 shows what can be judged a diagonal triangle leading to the September 6 high. Even though this peak was lower than that of March, it was only slightly lower, and because the formation is a diagonal triangle, which is always a fifth wave, one could argue that September 6 marked the orthodox top in what *Elliott Wave Principle* calls a truncation. (For a discussion of diagonal triangles and truncations, see Chapter 1 of *Elliott Wave Principle*.) In support of this interpretation of the pattern is the fact that the New York Composite index made its final high that same month (on September 1 basis the daily close and September 11 basis intraday extremes).

Each of the data points on the dates listed above represents what can be identified as the end of a wave pattern. Given the time relationships displayed in upcoming chapters, one is tempted to conclude that the market uses *all* such points in constructing its web of Fibonacci relationships. While these available options increase the odds of finding Fibonacci relationships, Chapter 13 and Appendices A, B and C will serve to show how little they matter in determining the success of a search.

## Calculating Durations in Days

Daily durations in this book are expressed as calendar days (not "trading days," when the market is open). They are meticulously calculated under the following regime: All years except "leap years" have 365 days, broken into months, as follows: J31, F28, M31, A30, M31, Jn30, Jy31, Au31, S30, O31, N30, D31. Each century, February has an extra day every fourth year beginning with the '04 year and every fourth '00 year beginning with the year zero. Here is a list of leap years from 1896 to date: 1896, 1904, 1908, 1912, 1916, 1920, 1924, 1928, 1932, 1936, 1940, 1944, 1948, 1952, 1956, 1960, 1964, 1968, 1972, 1976, 1980, 1984, 1988, 1992, 1996, 2000.

## Restrictions Due to Lack of Data

The illustrations in these studies use daily closing highs and lows in the Dow to determine the price extremes of waves and to mark the dates of wave terminations. With respect to exact moments that a wave ends, the Dow often makes its intraday turn the trading day before or after the daily closing extreme. This tendency gives each duration cited a leeway of at least plus or minus two days (one at each end). Also understand that sometimes a weekend and/or a holiday can intervene between the intraday and closing extremes, stretching that leeway out an additional two or three calendar days on each end of the duration. Similarly, the social mood could at times reach its extreme on a Saturday, Sunday or holiday, when the stock market is closed, in which case the actual date of the turn in psychology would be off from that of its meter, the stock market, by as much as three days. We must at least allow, for example, that the S&P's closing low of Friday, October 4, 1974 may have preceded the actual nadir of social mood on either of the following two weekend days. Then there are the rare times when a closing and intraday extreme are more than one day apart, such as the highs in the New York Composite cited above. With these uncertainties in mind, it is remarkable how often two durations on a daily closing basis are within one to four days of being related perfectly by a Fibonacci limit ratio. In the diagrams and calculations involving time, the fractions shown are often so close to .382 that there is no need to express them as squares of some decimal value for $\phi$ other than the limit ratio .618. Using actual intraday data, if we had it, might often have revealed perfection.

This report uses daily closes because prior to the employment of computers in calculating the intraday highs and lows for the Dow, record keepers created a "good enough" phony figure by adding all of the independent daily highs of the 30 DJIA stocks together. These so-called "theoretical" intraday highs and lows for the DJIA are different from the daily highs and lows that the average actually recorded. This fault makes it impossible to use historical "intraday" prices in computations for the averages, because they are false. Even the *dates* of the market's intraday turns on this basis are suspect, because the date of a "theoretical" intraday high need not be the same as the date of the intraday high for the average. Recent experience nevertheless shows that they are identical in many cases. If you would like to re-do all the time-related illustrations in this report using the dates of intraday extremes, I would be happy first to send you my condolences and later to review and perhaps publish the results.

**Chapter 5**

# PRICE RELATIONSHIPS WITHIN SUPERCYCLE WAVE (V)

*Figure 5-1:*

## Wave V from 1982

As discussed in Chapter 3, R.N. Elliott observed in the 1940s that the most reliable relationship in a completed wave with a fifth-wave extension is that the gain of wave five will be related by the Fibonacci ratio to the total gain of waves one through three. In Supercycle wave (V), waves I-III took place from 1932 to 1966. The rise in terms of daily closing price extremes created a multiple of just over 24 times. Wave V from 1982 to 2000 created a multiple of just over 15 times. Note that this relationship is 8 to 5. In other words, wave V produced **5/8** of the multiple of waves I-III, as shown in Figure 5-1.

This relationship is very nearly exact. If we take the multiple of waves I though III out to four (or more) decimal places at 24.1424, and multiply it by 5/8, or .625, and project an upside target from its starting point at 776.92, we get **11,722.95**. The all-time closing high on January 14, 2000 was **11,722.98**. We can further appreciate how close these numbers are by understanding that the smallest possible incremental DJIA change that a single stock within the average could produce at the time was 0.31 Dow point, which is ten times the difference between the two numbers! It took an intricate cooperation among Dow issues to achieve a reading that was essentially a perfect Fibonacci number fraction. Thus, wave V from 1982 has satisfied Elliott's targeting observation of sixty years ago by fulfilling a precise Fibonacci relationship to the net rise of the preceding two impulse waves. In fact, it reflects the *specific* Fibonacci relationship embodied in the idealized illustration added to *Elliott Wave Principle* a dozen years ago, as reproduced in Figure 3-5, which is marked "⑤ =.618 ①–③."

There are two additional mathematical curiosities worth noting. The precise multiple for wave V is 15.0890, where the Fibonacci number 89 follows the decimal point. The precise multiple for waves I-III is 24.1424, where the Fibonacci number 144 is (almost) the number that follows the decimal point. The apparent reason that the second decimal portion is not *exactly* 144 is that 142.4 is 8/5 of 89. Thus, the *offset* from whole numbers shares

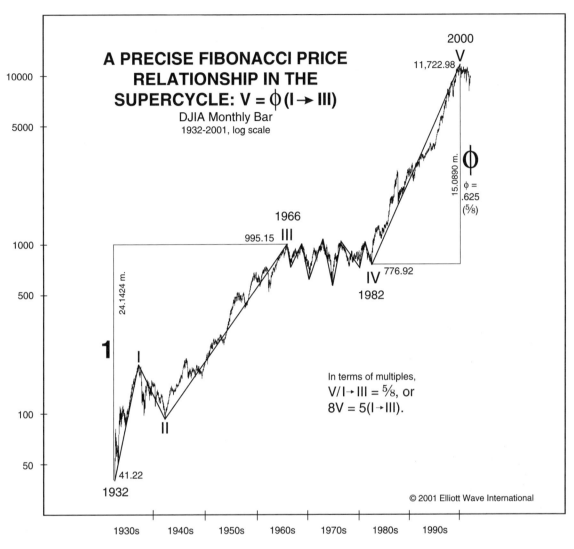

**A PRECISE FIBONACCI PRICE RELATIONSHIP IN THE SUPERCYCLE: V = φ (I → III)**
DJIA Monthly Bar
1932-2001, log scale

2000
V
11,722.98

φ
φ = .625 (⅝)

15.0890 m.

1966
995.15 III

IV 776.92
1982

24.1424 m.

1

I

II

In terms of multiples,
V/I→III = ⅝, or
8V = 5(I→III).

41.22
1932

© 2001 Elliott Wave International

1930s 1940s 1950s 1960s 1970s 1980s 1990s

*Figure 5-1*

exactly the same Fibonacci relationship that the whole numbers themselves do. This is why the entire decimal expressions, 24.1424 and 15.0890, are in 8/5 ratio. As we will see in Figures 6-5 and 6-6, the 5/8 ratio governs the same set of waves within Cycle wave V. *These are precisely the sets of waves between which R.N. Elliott told us, 55 years ago, to expect a Fibonacci relationship.* The market took 68 years crafting this picture, so take your time soaking it in.

## *Figure 5-2:*

## Waves V and I-III Expressed as Whole Numbers

Figure 5-2 shows the same picture but expressed in whole number multiples of a shared factor. The factor shared by 24.1424 and 15.0890 is the number 3.0178. This means that waves I-III have achieved approximately 8 times a triple, and wave V has achieved approximately 5 times a triple. The multiples have thus managed to involve three sequential Fibonacci numbers: 3, 5 and 8, in creating the two multiples of its major price relationship.

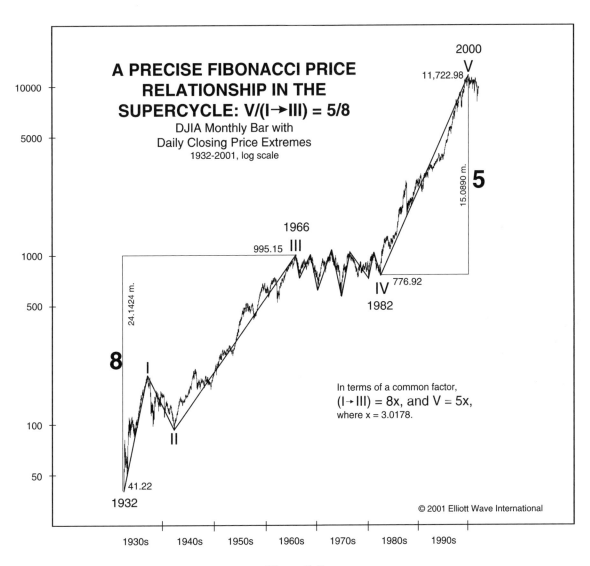

**A PRECISE FIBONACCI PRICE
RELATIONSHIP IN THE
SUPERCYCLE: V/(I→III) = 5/8**
DJIA Monthly Bar with
Daily Closing Price Extremes
1932-2001, log scale

2000
V
11,722.98

5
15.0890 m.

1966
995.15    III

IV    776.92
1982

24.1424 m.

8

I

II

In terms of a common factor,
(I→III) = 8x, and V = 5x,
where x = 3.0178.

41.22
1932

© 2001 Elliott Wave International

1930s   1940s   1950s   1960s   1970s   1980s   1990s

10000
5000
1000
500
100
50

*Figure 5-2*

### Figure 5-3:

## Wave V from 1974

Wave V is related not only to waves I-III but also to wave I, fulfilling the other measuring guideline as well. This time, the measurement for wave V is taken from the other acceptable low, in 1974. As you can see in Figure 5-3, wave V's multiple is $1.6266^3$ times that of wave I. Phi in this case is within 0.10 percent of the fraction **13/8** (1.625). An exact relationship of $(13/8)^3$ would target 11,689.06, which is off the actual high by only 34 points, or less than 1/3 of one percent.

V/I, which is 4.3035, is approximately 13/3. In other words, I/3 = V/13. The factor shared by waves I and V is the number 1.5667 ± .0055, which encompasses the fraction 11/7 (1.5714) and is about half of the value of the factor for the waves in Figure 5-1.

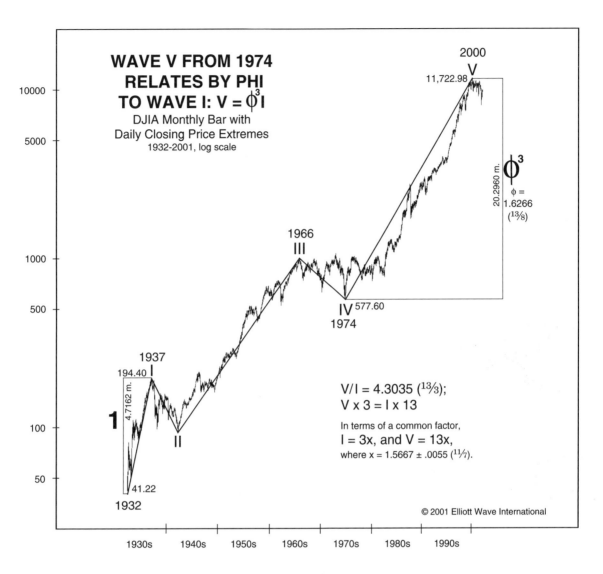

*Figure 5-3*

## Figure 5-4:

## Wave V from 1974 and 1982

Figure 5-4 shows the combined picture for wave V over a 68-year period. Cycle wave V has achieved Fibonacci relationships using both measuring guidelines, relating by $\phi$ to waves I-III and by $\phi^3$ to wave I. These relationships pay tribute to both acceptable starting points for wave V, i.e., 1974 and 1982. Mass psychology has produced a mathematical work of art, satisfying both of the measuring guidelines that R.N. Elliott formulated over half a century ago.

The market's dual mathematical achievement over a period of 68 years is not likely due to chance, for two reasons: Wave practitioners described in advance the two sets of waves that are typically related by Fibonacci, and the relationships were met with striking precision. Furthermore, these were not the only Fibonacci relationships that occurred, as ensuing figures demonstrate.

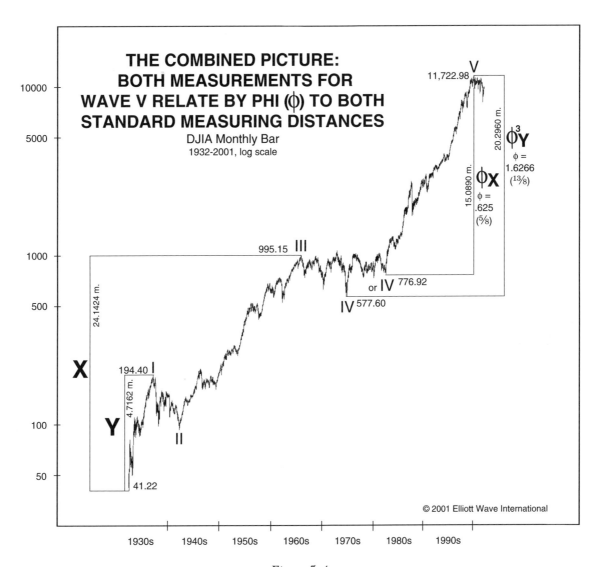

**THE COMBINED PICTURE:**
**BOTH MEASUREMENTS FOR**
**WAVE V RELATE BY PHI (φ) TO BOTH**
**STANDARD MEASURING DISTANCES**

DJIA Monthly Bar
1932-2001, log scale

© 2001 Elliott Wave International

*Figure 5-4*

*Figure 5-5:*

## The Combined Relationships Utilize Four Consecutive Fibonacci Numbers

The fractions in Figures 5-1 and 5-3 utilize four consecutive Fibonacci numbers: 3, 5, 8 and 13. Figure 5-5 shows them together. The 5/8 relationship is exact; the 3/13 ratio is off by 0.7 percent.

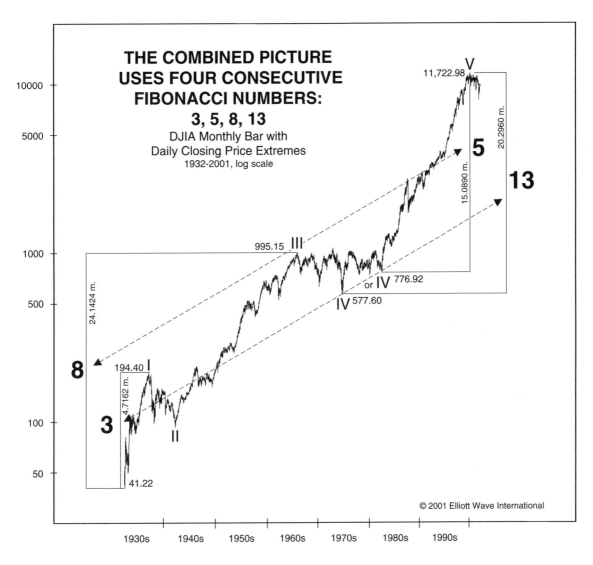

*Figure 5-5*

*Figure 5-6:*

## Waves I-III Relate by Phi to the Entire Supercycle

Waves I-III relate by Fibonacci to the length of the entire Supercycle. This relationship is not precise with respect to powers of a Fibonacci-number fraction but is very close to $(18/11)^5$. Given the high power and the deviation from an ideal fraction, this relationship is not satisfying. As we will see in Figure 5-13, however, the individual motive waves (I, III and V) relate to wave (V) in a remarkable progression of Fibonacci fractions and powers.

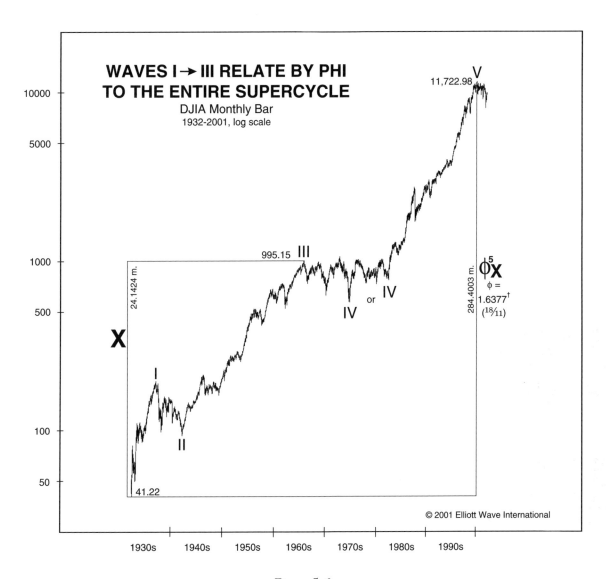

**WAVES I → III RELATE BY PHI TO THE ENTIRE SUPERCYCLE**

DJIA Monthly Bar

1932-2001, log scale

© 2001 Elliott Wave International

*Figure 5-6*

## *Figure 5-7:*

## Wave III Relates by Phi to Five Major Advances

Wave III proves to be another measuring unit, which has a nearly perfect Fibonacci relationship to wave I and to waves I-III. As you can see in Figure 5-7, wave III relates to wave I by $(2/3)^2$ and to waves I-III by $(3/2)^2$! So wave III is a perfect median between our two original measuring waves.

Figure 5-7 further shows that wave III has a nearly perfect Fibonacci relationship to the portion of wave V ending in 1987 and to Primary wave ⑤ from 1987. As Figure 5-13 demonstrates, wave III is also related by phi to the entire Supercycle. All five of these fractional relationships are so close that to three decimal places, they are each off by 3/1000 or less. The actual ratios are 1.502, .664, .620 and 1.598. The corresponding Fibonacci fractions are 3/2, 2/3, 13/21 and 8/5, which have decimal expressions of 1.5, .667, .619 and 1.6.

(The calculation for Primary wave ⑤ uses the orthodox low in 1987, which occurred on December 4. The price low occurred on October 19 at 1738.74. Using that low gives a multiple of 6.7422 and a ratio to wave III of .6295, which is 17/27.)

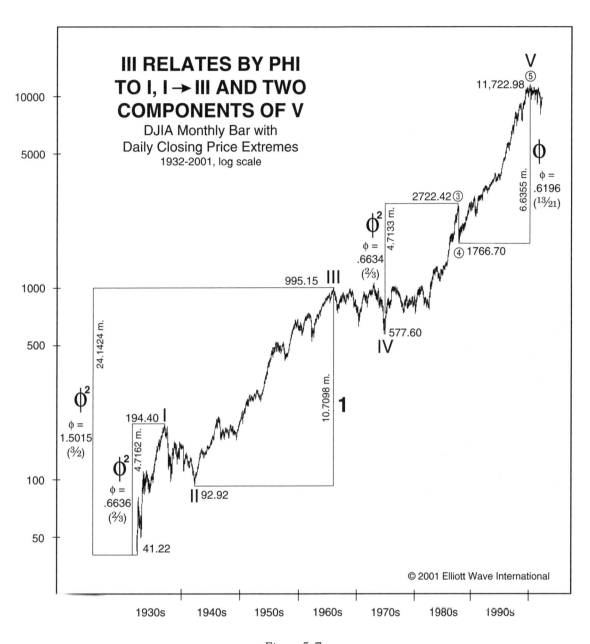

*Figure 5-7*

*Figure 5-8:*

## How the Measuring Waves Relate to Each Other and to Wave III

The two measuring units, waves I and I-III, are related as 3 is to 2, to the fourth power. As already shown in Figure 5-7, these advances, labeled X and Y, also relate to wave III, as $X = (3/2)^2III$, and $Y = (2/3)^2III$.

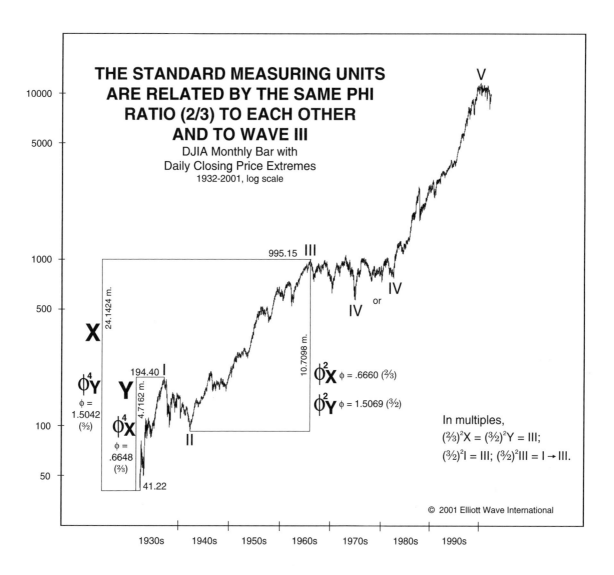

*Figure 5-8*

*Figure 5-9:*

## Waves II and IV to 1974 Each Relate by Phi to a Measuring Unit

Wave II relates by $\phi^5$ to waves I-III, and wave IV relates by $\phi^2$ to wave I. The two $\phi$ values are outside our narrow range for acceptability but very close to "Fibonacci" ratios of non-Fibonacci numbers.

Figure 5-7 showed that wave III is a $\phi^2$ median multiple between wave I and waves I-III. Figures 5-6 and 5-9 show that waves I-III play the same role at a $\phi^5$ multiple with respect to wave II and to the entire Supercycle. The former multiple is related by $\phi^5$, the latter by $1/\phi^5$, where $\phi = .6131$ and $.6106$, respectively, which is $.6118 \pm .0013$. While these ratios fall outside our narrow range for phi, their near-equality makes them interesting.

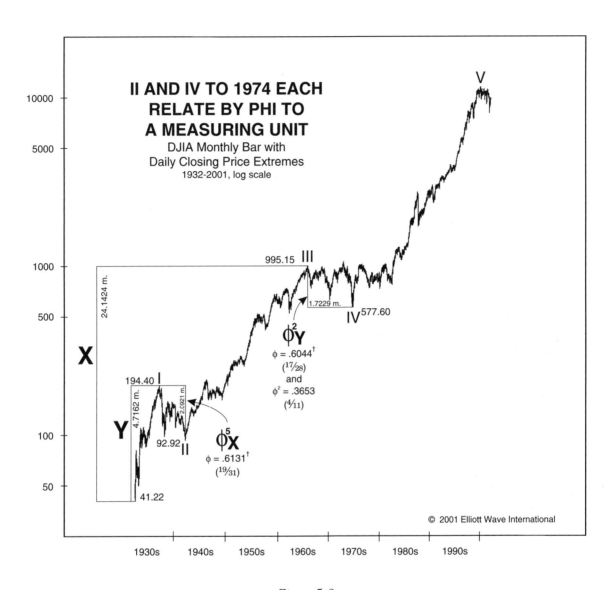

*Figure 5-9*

## *Figure 5-10:*

## Waves II and IV to 1982 Relate to Previous Waves and to Each Other by .613

Figure 5-9 showed that wave II is related by $\phi^5$ to waves I-III, and this chart additionally shows that wave IV to 1982 is related by $\phi^6$ to waves I-III. The Fibonacci root in both cases is .613. Coextensively, waves II and IV are themselves related by essentially the same number, .6123. In other words, II=(19/31)$^5$X, IV=(19/31)$^6$X, and IV=(19/31)II, a striking set of relationships for the two corrective waves. The text accompanying Figure 5-13 will cite yet another 9/31 relationship.

The expression $\phi^6$X, where $\phi$ = .6130, can also be written $(\phi^2)^3$X, where $\phi^2$ = .3758, which is very close to 3/8, or $(\phi^3)^2$X, where $\phi^3$ = .2303, which is very close to 3/13. Thus, although the $\phi$ factor for this expression is not within acceptable range, the $\phi^2$ and $\phi^3$ factors are.

The fact that wave IV has two endings gives it two measurements. Figures 5-9 and 5-10 show that one of those measurements is $\phi^2$I, and the other is $\phi$II.

Figure 5-10 is a more satisfying picture than Figure 5-9. Along with Figure 5-1, it offers evidence that the market's relationships take into account the 1982 low as a candidate for the end of wave IV.

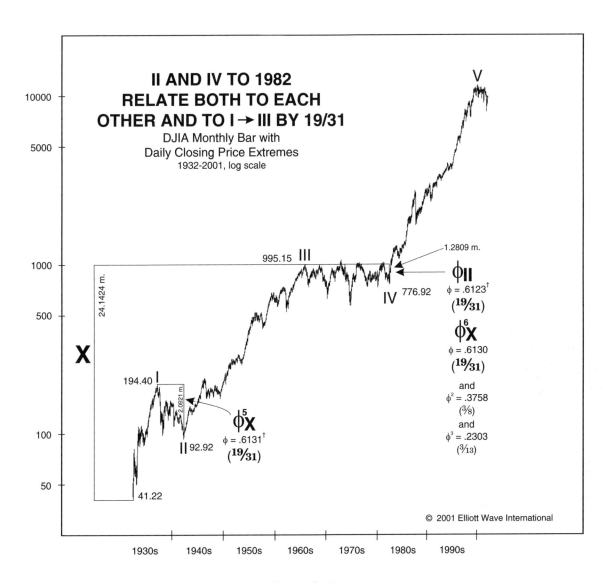

**II AND IV TO 1982
RELATE BOTH TO EACH
OTHER AND TO I → III BY 19/31**
DJIA Monthly Bar with
Daily Closing Price Extremes
1932-2001, log scale

© 2001 Elliott Wave International

*Figure 5-10*

### Figure 5-11:

## Wave V to the 1987 High

Long term subscribers will recall that wave V gave a precise nod of recognition to the second wave-measuring guideline when it topped in 1987. Wave V from 1974 would have equalled the multiple of wave I at a daily closing high of 2723.96. The daily closing high on August 25, 1987 was 2722.42, off by a mere point and a half. It led directly to a 1000-point fall in less than two months. EWT's "sell signal" of October 5, 1987, the day before the 900-point crash began, was based partly upon this relationship. Even though wave V did not end there, it was clear that the Dow respected that measuring guideline.

As you can see in Figure 5-11, this equality occurred when measuring wave V from the 1974 low. From the 1982 low, the rise to the 1987 high relates to the ultimate gain of wave V by a Fibonacci ratio, 4.3061, which is only 0.12 percent from the Fibonacci fraction, 13/3. This multiple is $\phi^3$, where $\phi$ is 1.6269, or 13/8. Turn back to Figure 5-4 and notice that this is precisely the same relationship that wave V from the 1974 low holds to wave I. So regardless of which starting point we use (1974 or 1982, or even 1980), the total multiple of wave V is $\phi^3$ times the rise of wave V to 1987, where $\phi \approx 1.6269$. Further, the total multiple of waves I-III is $\phi^4$ times the rise of wave V from 1982 to 1987, where $\phi$ is 1.6201, which is only 0.06 percent from 34/21.

When measuring wave V as a $\phi^3$ multiple of its rise from 1982 to 1987, an exact 13/8 ratio for $\phi$ would target 11,682, 41 points from the actual high. A difference of only 2.72 points at the 1982 starting level would have made the relationship perfect at the actual high. The market's action on the week of that bottom seems to suggest that it respected this difference. Our starting point for measurement is the daily closing low in 1982, which occurred on Friday, August 12 at 776.92. On Tuesday, August 9, an hourly low was registered a few points lower, at 774.54, almost exactly (0.34 above) where that ideal starting point would be. The intraday low of the average, if it were available, would surely be a bit lower than that and closer to the ideal 774.20. The "leeway" allowed for our fractions may in fact be little more than a matter of lacking precise data.

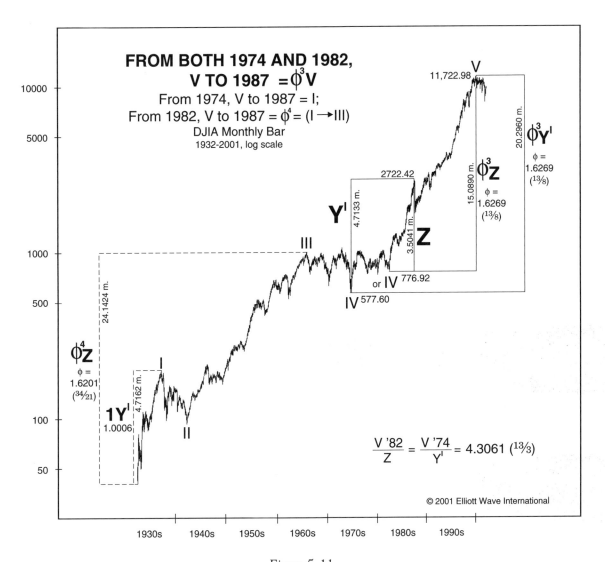

**FROM BOTH 1974 AND 1982,**
**V TO 1987 = $\phi^3$V**

From 1974, V to 1987 = I;
From 1982, V to 1987 = $\phi^4$ = (I →III)
DJIA Monthly Bar
1932-2001, log scale

$$\frac{V\ '82}{Z} = \frac{V\ '74}{Y^I} = 4.3061\ (^{13}/_3)$$

© 2001 Elliott Wave International

*Figure 5-11*

### Figure 5-12:

## A Panorama

Figure 5-12 shows that all major phases of advance and retrenchment from 1932 to the year 2000 are related by Fibonacci multiples to one of our two measuring waves, denoted X and Y, which are themselves related by $\phi^4$, where $\phi = 3/2$.

This graph plus Figures 5-7 and 5-10 show all the Fibonacci ratios found among the components of Supercycle wave (V).

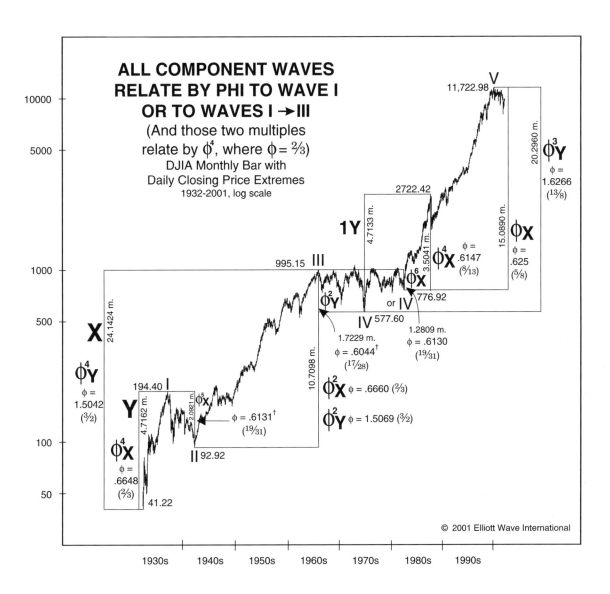

*Figure 5-12*

*Figure 5-13*

## Component Motive Waves Are Related to the Entire Supercycle by Consecutive Powers of Consecutive Fibonacci-Number Ratios

No one has postulated that components of a wave must be related to the entire wave. Nor may we too readily make such a claim, because the relationships between waves that differ in size involve high powers of phi, so finding them may not be a particularly low probability. The ones that exist for this structure, however, are quite precise expressions of Fibonacci-number ratios, and they form a consecutive progression of fractions and powers. Figure 5-13 presents, to five decimal places, the relationships between the entire wave (V) and sub-waves I, III and V, using the 1980 starting point for wave V (see Appendix B). In the first two cases, the difference from an ideal ratio is identical at .16 percent. In the third case, it is exact to four decimal places. (This is true whether we use 759.13 or 759.98 for the orthodox closing low; see Appendix B for a discussion of the difference.) Here are the primary observations:

—Wave I is related to wave (V) by $(.59904)^8$. The root is very close to **3/5** (.60000).
—Wave III is related to wave (V) by $(.62597)^7$. The root is very close to **5/8** (.62500).
—Wave (V) is related to wave V by $(.61536)^6$. The root is almost exactly **8/13** (.61538).
—The ratios are **3/5**, **5/8** and **8/13**, which are consecutive Fibonacci number ratios, and the powers are the **eighth**, **seventh** and **sixth**, which are consecutive powers! This dual progression strongly suggests an ordering principle at work. Now look back at Figure 5-6 and see that waves I-III, the largest measuring unit, relate to the Supercycle by 11/18 to the **fifth** power, the next power in the progression.

That this progression uses the 1980 low for wave V further justifies earlier published commentary that the 1980 low is an acceptable end of wave IV from the standpoint of wave form. Most Fibonacci relationships involving wave V measure from the 1974 or 1982 low, however, so it is more satisfying overall to begin wave V in one of those years.

Here are a few additional observations, not shown in Figure 5-13:
—Wave V from 1982 is also related to wave (V), by $(.6130)^6$, which is $(19/31)^6$. As shown in Figure 10, 19/31 is the same root that governs three other wave relationships, and one of them is also to the sixth power! To summarize the list, V'82/(V) = $(19/31)^6$, IV/X = $(19/31)^6$, II/X = $(19/31)^5$, and IV/II = 19/31. Again, while this ratio is outside our boundaries for $\phi$, it can be expressed as $(3/8)^3$ or $(3/13)^2$, each of which is within bounds.

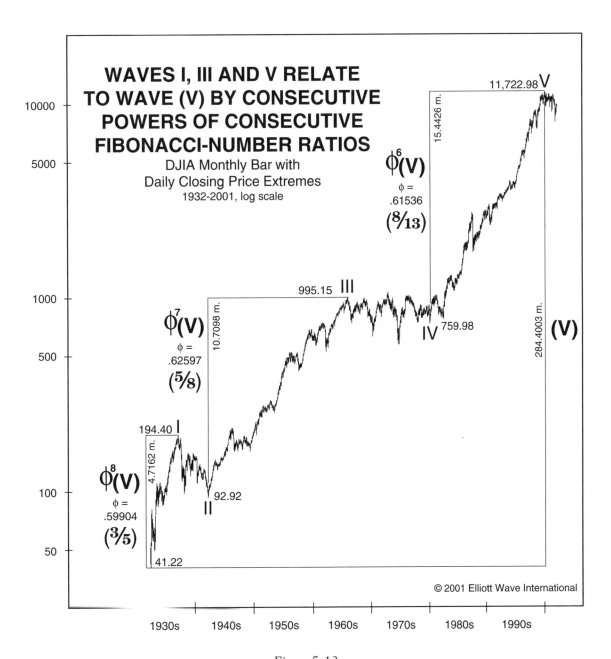

*Figure 5-13*

—The measuring unit (waves I-III, denoted X in previous illustrations) is related to wave (V) by $(.6106)^5$ (which is .08 percent from 11/18). Referring back to Figure 5-9 or 5-10, note that X has almost the same relationship to wave II, inverted, which is $(.6131)^5$. Stated succinctly, $X/(V) = II/X = (.612 \pm .001)^5$. While the decimal is outside our boundaries for an acceptable Fibonacci number ratio, this duality is interesting.

—Wave V from the 1974 low is related to wave (V) by $(9/14)^6$. The decimal, .6440 (which is .18 percent from 9/14), is outside our boundaries.

—Wave (V) is related to all measurements for wave V (from 1974, 1980 and 1982) by the sixth power of phi.

Figure 5-13 prompts a tentative generalization that an entire motive wave may be related by powers of phi to each of its motive components. (The corrective waves, II and IV, are also related to (V) by powers of phi, but the powers are so high that any inferences would be unwarranted.)

# Chapter 6

# *PRICE RELATIONSHIPS WITHIN CYCLE WAVE V*

### *Figures 6-1 and 6-2:*

## Wave ⑤ is in Phi Relationship to Waves ①-③, in Two Ways

Wave ③ has two acceptable tops, those of April 6 and August 25, 1987. *The Elliott Wave Theorist* discussed these two junctures years ago. For a close-up view, see Figures 4-4 and 4-5.

Taking our first measuring unit, waves ①-③, as ending on April 6, 1987, we find that wave ⑤ is related to waves ①-③ by the Fibonacci ratio in two ways, using the two best starting dates for wave V and the two best starting dates for wave ⑤. (See discussion in Chapter 4.) Figure 6-1 shows the φ relationship using the 1974 and 1987 lows, and Figure 6-2 shows the 5/8 relationship using the 1982 and 1990 lows. Each of these ratios is so precise that they are off by only .0004 and .0003 respectively.

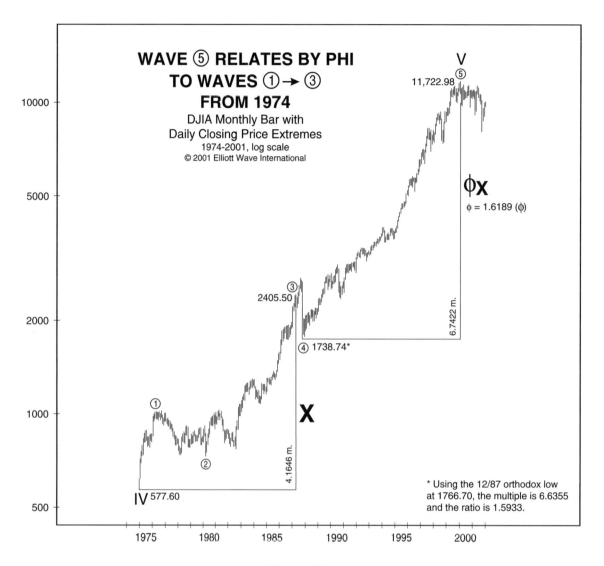

*Figure 6-1*

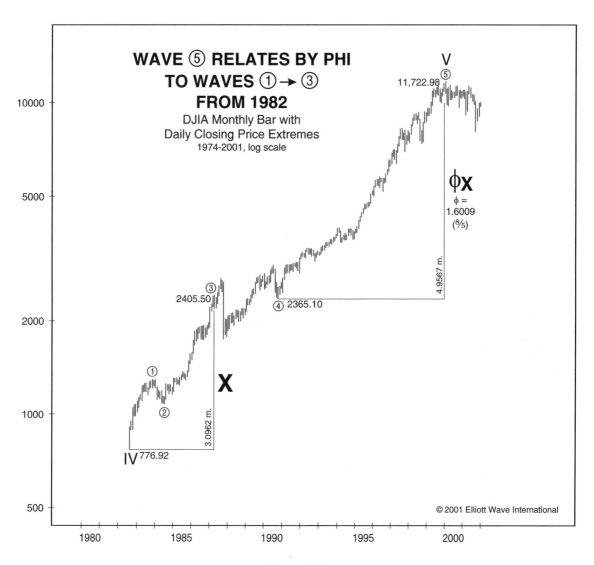

*Figure 6-2*

## *Figure 6-3:*

## The Combined Picture

Figure 6-3 combines the observations from Figures 6-1 and 6-2. It displays the amazing utility of these two sets of lows in creating a Fibonacci relationship in both sets of multiples, where the smaller set is related by .625 (5/8), and the larger set is related by .618 ($\phi$).

Recall from Figures 4-4 and 4-5 in Chapter 4 that the 1987 low had a price low in October and an orthodox low in December, at 1738.74 and 1766.74 respectively. Using the latter low, the ratio for the larger set of multiples is .628. The .618 and .628 ratios from those two lows appear as a compromise to an in-between number that would generate close to a 5/8 ratio identical to that of the smaller set of multiples.

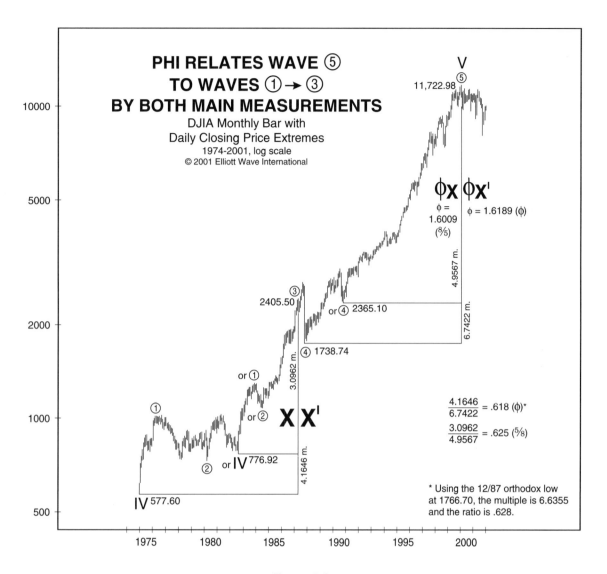

**PHI RELATES WAVE ⑤**
**TO WAVES ① → ③**
**BY BOTH MAIN MEASUREMENTS**
DJIA Monthly Bar with
Daily Closing Price Extremes
1974-2001, log scale
© 2001 Elliott Wave International

$$\frac{4.1646}{6.7422} = .618\ (\phi)^*$$

$$\frac{3.0962}{4.9567} = .625\ (\tfrac{5}{8})$$

\* Using the 12/87 orthodox low
at 1766.70, the multiple is 6.6355
and the ratio is .628.

*Figure 6-3*

*Figure 6-4:*

## Wave ⑤ is to ①-③ as Wave V is to I-III

These illustrations place the precise relationship shown in Figure 5-1 together with the relationship in Figure 6-2. When labeling the end of wave IV in 1982, the corresponding components of waves (V) and V both subdivide into an 8/5 ratio. In other words, the very same numbers, **5** and **8**, govern the main targeting relationship for the fifth and final wave in both the Cycle and the Supercycle. As discussed along with Figure 5-1, the ratio is so close to perfection in the Supercycle that a projection on this basis projects an upside target of 11,722.95, off by only 0.03 in the DJIA. The ratio is nearly as close in Cycle wave V. To four decimal places, the ratio is 1.6009. Applying an 8/5, or 1.6000, ratio to the measuring unit's multiple projects an upside target of 11,716.52, which is off from the actual high by only 6.46 points. Clearly, the DJIA had 5/8 and 8/5 in mind when it registered its final high at 11,722.98 on January 14, 2000.

Notice in Figure 6-4 that waves ④ and IV contain higher prices than the peaks of waves ③ and III respectively and end at orthodox lows that are above their price lows. Thus, there are similarities in both form and ratios.

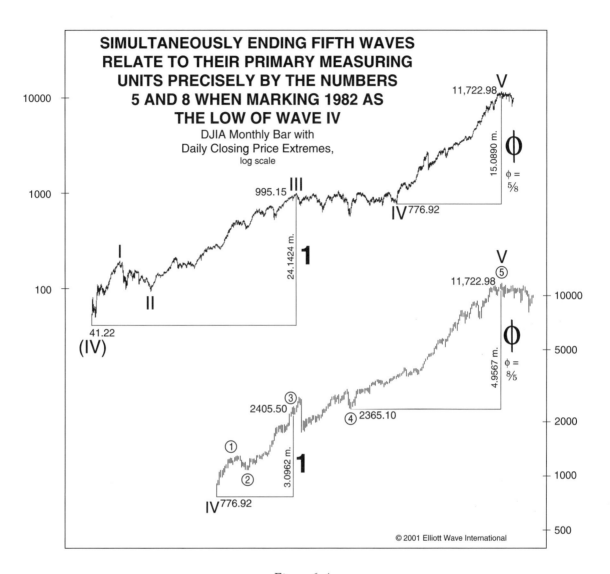

Figure 6-4

*Figure 6-5:*

## The Ratios Shown as Fibonacci Multiples

Figure 6-5 shows the relationships of Figure 6-1 as multiples of a common factor. In this case, the common factor for the waves within Cycle V is .62, an expression of the Fibonacci ratio.

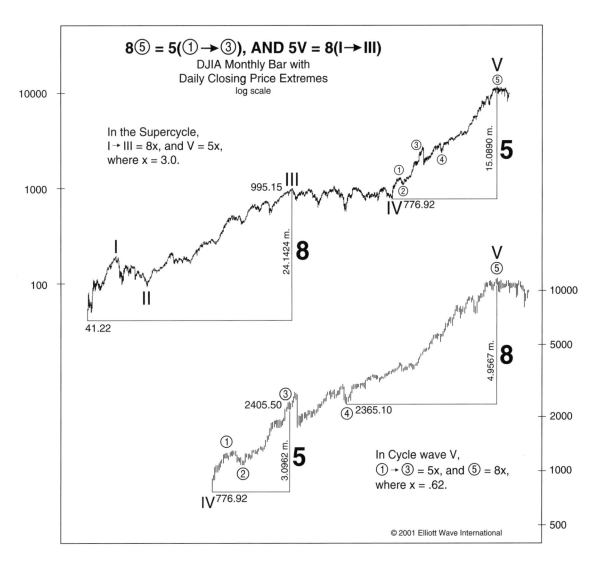

Figure 6-5

*Figure 6-6:*

## The Multiples on One Price Series

Figure 6-6 places the dual relationship between wave five and waves one through three on a single price series.

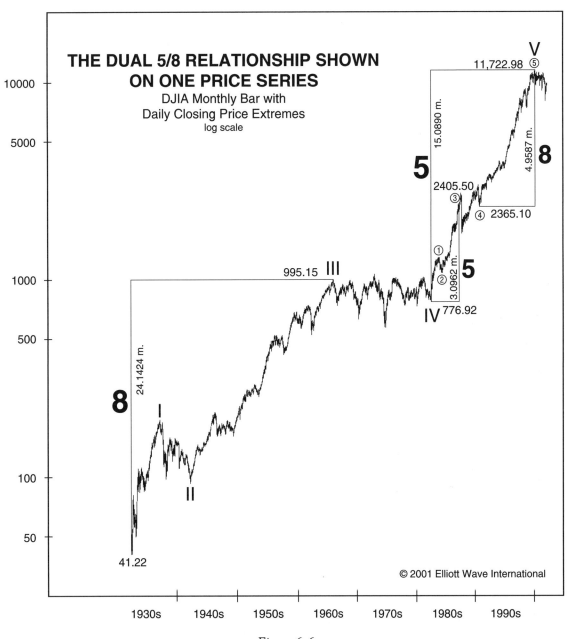

THE DUAL 5/8 RELATIONSHIP SHOWN
ON ONE PRICE SERIES
DJIA Monthly Bar with
Daily Closing Price Extremes
log scale

© 2001 Elliott Wave International

*Figure 6-6*

**Figure 6-7:**

## Waves ①-③ and ⑤ Are in $\phi^2$ Relationship to Wave ①

Figure 6-7 shows that the multiple of wave ⑤ is $\phi^2$ times that of wave ①. Measuring wave ⑤ from October 1990 gives a $\phi$ value of 1.6797, which is close to 5/3. Measuring wave ⑤ from January 1991 gives a $\phi$ value of 1.6435, which is close to 28/17. Both of these values are slightly out of our acceptable range for Fibonacci ratios, but it may be of interest that their average to five decimal places is 0.30 percent from 5/3.

Thus, wave ⑤, like wave V (see Figure 5-4), is related by Fibonacci to both of its primary measuring units. In Cycle wave V, the sub-waves are related by equality and $\phi^2$; in the Supercycle, they are related by $\phi$ and $\phi^3$.

Wave ⑤'s multiple is approximately equal to that of waves ①-③, which makes the latter also $\phi^2$ times the multiple for wave ①. Here the root of $\phi^2$ falls outside our narrow range of acceptability for $\phi$, although it is close to 18/11.

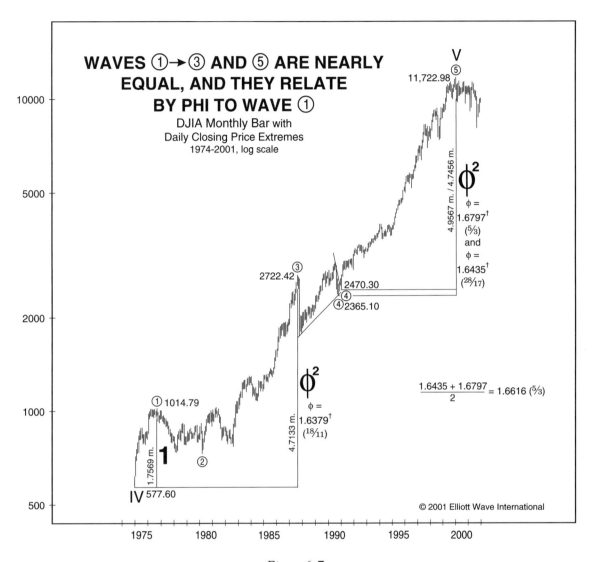

*Figure 6-7*

## *Figure 6-8:*

## The Dual Wave One/Five Relationship

Figure 6-8 places the relationship shown between waves one and five in Figure 5-3 together with that shown in Figure 6-7.

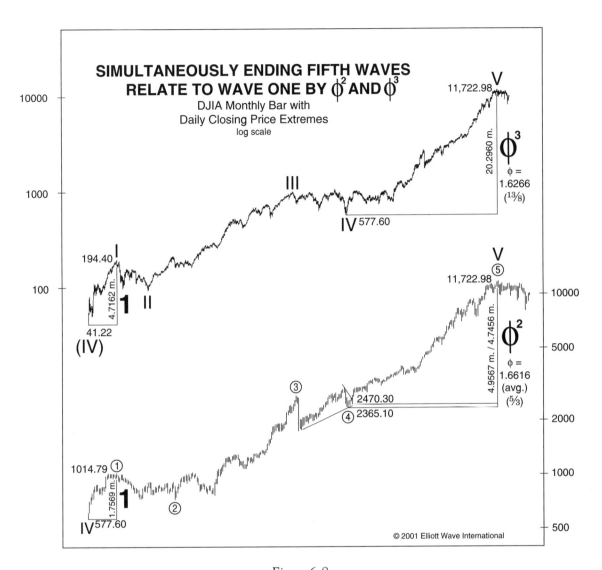

*Figure 6-8*

### *Figure 6-9:*

## The Ratios Shown as Fibonacci Multiples

Figure 6-9 shows the same idea in terms of Fibonacci fractions, although these ratios fall outside our tight ranges. The number 3 represents both first waves. The fifth wave of the Cycle is represented by 8, and the fifth wave of the Supercycle is represented by 13.

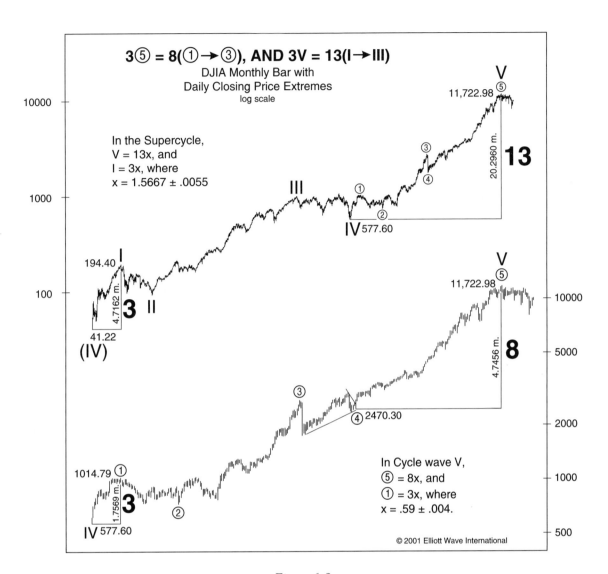

Figure 6-9

*Figure 6-10:*

## The Multiples on One Price Series

Figure 6-10 places the dual wave one/wave five relationship on a single price series. While this is an intriguing picture, it lacks the exceptional elegance and precision of Figure 6-6.

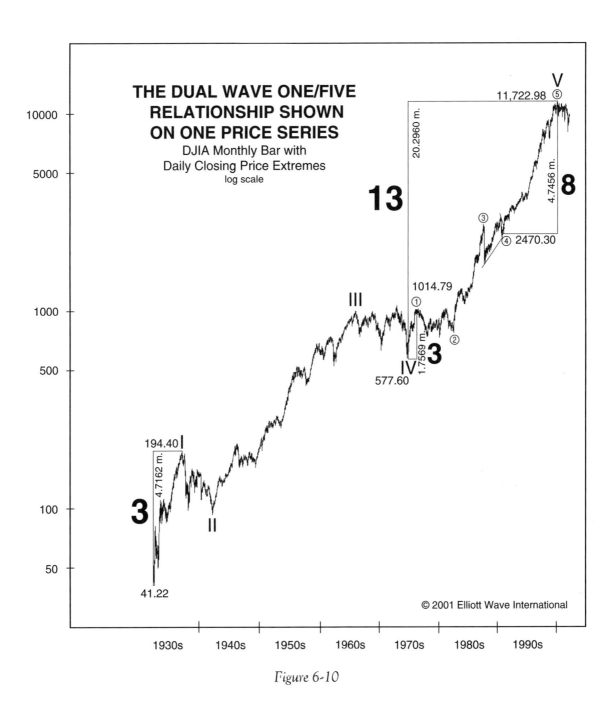

**THE DUAL WAVE ONE/FIVE
RELATIONSHIP SHOWN
ON ONE PRICE SERIES**
DJIA Monthly Bar with
Daily Closing Price Extremes
log scale

© 2001 Elliott Wave International

Figure 6-10

## Figure 6-11:

## The Combined Picture: Wave ⑤'s Phi Relationships to Both Measuring Units

Figure 6-11 shows all three of wave ⑤'s Fibonacci relationships to the measuring units that are typically used to target fifth waves.

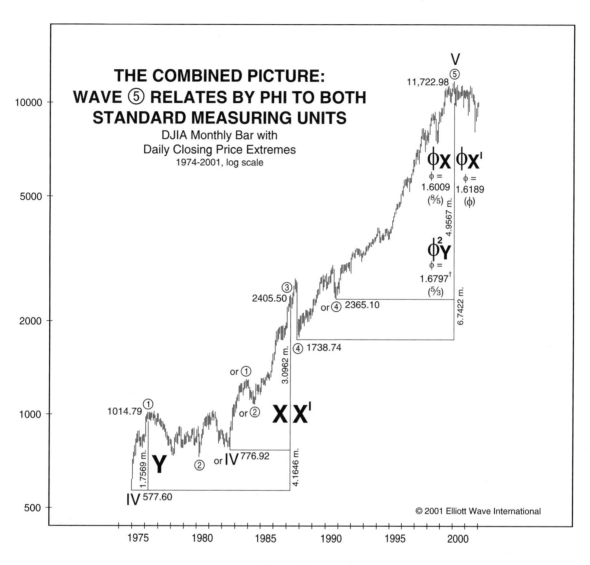

Figure 6-11

*Figure 6-12:*

## Wave ⑤ Relates by Phi to Wave ③ in Two Ways

The multiples of wave ⑤ from 1990 and 1991 relate by various values of $\phi$ to the multiples of wave ③ from 1978, 1980 and 1982. Figure 6-12 shows two ways in which ⑤/③ produces a Fibonacci number fraction, namely 3/2 and 8/5. In both cases, they are nearly exact. The 8/5 relationship is shown in a different context in Figures 6-2 and 6-11.

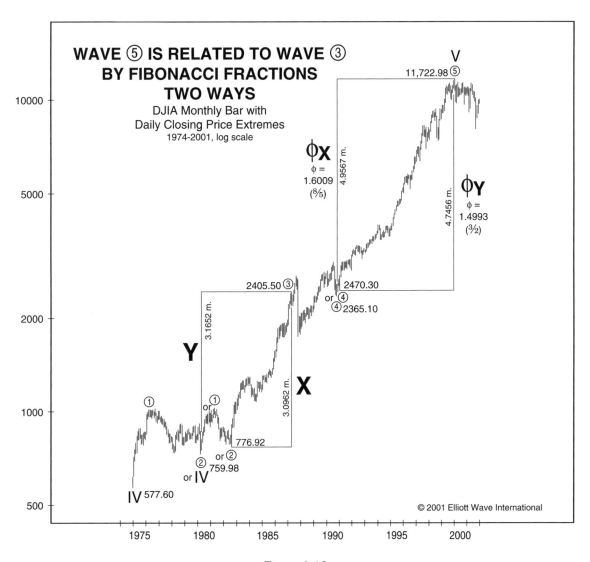

*Figure 6-12*

*Figure 6-13:*

## Wave ⑤ Relates by the Same Ratio to Wave ③ in Two Ways

Figure 6-13 shows a short and long measurement for wave ③ and wave ⑤ so that both multiples between them are the same, 1.53, which is between 3/2 and 14/9. This ratio is outside our tight guidelines, but the identical result makes it interesting. Tables 4-K and 4-L counts this ratio once because had the ratios between the two sets of waves not been equal, I would have no reason to mention them at all.

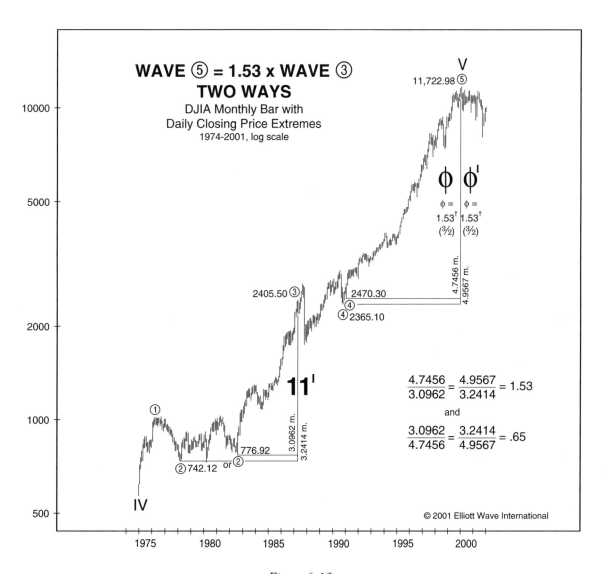

*Figure 6-13*

## *Figure 6-14:*

### Wave ④ Equals Wave ②

There are a number of ways to measure waves ② and ④. Wave ②'s maximum travel (to the 1978 low) produces approximately the same multiple as does wave ④ from its orthodox high in April 1987 to its orthodox low in December 1987. The difference between them is 0.43 percent.

As mentioned in Chapter 4, the 1978 low is the end of wave ② in the S&P, but in the Dow, the end of wave ② is more properly labeled in 1980 in terms of wave form. A few figures in this book show a "wave ②" label at the 1978 low in the Dow for the convenience of observing the associated multiples. This notation should be understood as meaning "the lowest *daily close* within wave ②." The apparent disparity between the two points does not constitute any kind of theoretical problem because the *intraday* low in 1980 was lower than that in 1978 even though the daily closing low was not. If intraday readings were available for these studies, we would naturally use the lower value at the 1980 low, not the higher one at the 1978 low, keeping the price multiples for wave ② in accordance with the wave labels. I also suspect that such multiples would be even closer to satisfying the illustrated relationships.

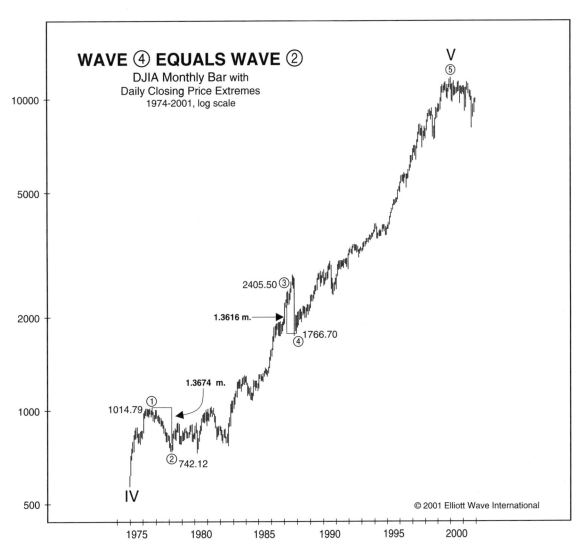

*Figure 6-14*

# Chapter 7

# *PRICE CROSS-RELATIONSHIPS BETWEEN WAVES V AND (V)*

*Figure 7-1:*

## All Advancing Waves in Cycle V and in Supercycle (V) are Cross-Related By Ratios Between Alternate Fibonacci Numbers ($\phi^2$)

In terms of multiples, wave ③ has the same relationship to wave III as wave ⑤ has to wave V, i.e., 1/3. Wave ① is related to wave I by 3/8, which is likewise a ratio between alternate Fibonacci numbers.

All of these lengths use extreme price points. Using an orthodox low in *April* 1980 (see the opening discussion in Appendix B) at 759.98 improves the ③/III ratio slightly to .3345.

Using the 1982 and 1990 lows for the start of waves V and ⑤ respectively (not shown), ⑤/V=.3285, which is 1.4% from 1/3 but hints of an attempt. The square root of .3285 is .5731, which is close to 4/7.

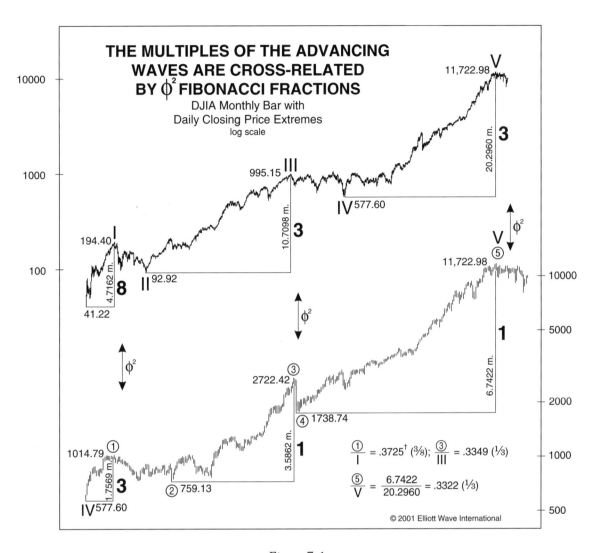

*Figure 7-1*

*Figure 7-2:*

## Both Corrections in Cycle V and Supercycle (V) Are Cross-Related by Ratios Between Adjacent Fibonacci Numbers (φ)

While the advancing waves are cross-related by $\phi^2$ (see Figure 7-1), the corrective waves are cross-related by $\phi$. Specifically, ②/II = .6246 (5/8), and ④/IV = .6681 (2/3).

Measuring wave ② from the orthodox top of wave ① at 1004.65 on December 31, 1976 gives a multiple of 1.2931, in which case, ②/II = .618, the phi limit ratio. Using the other two acceptable lows for wave ② (742.12 and 759.13) and the two highs for wave ① yields ratios between .633 and .654.

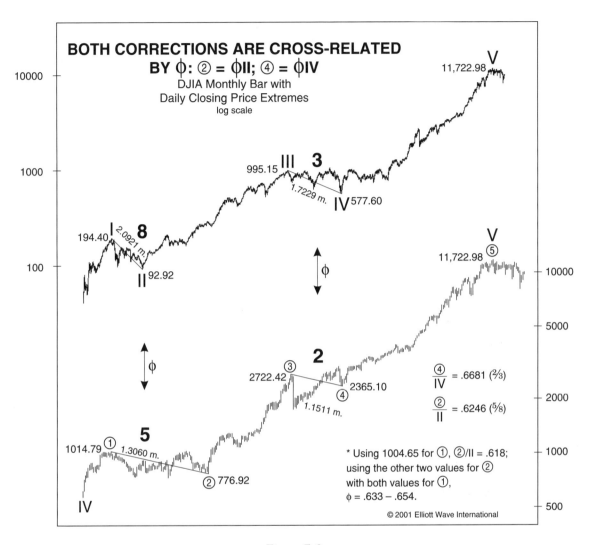

*Figure 7-2*

*Figure 7-3:*

## The Combined Picture: Advances and Corrections Are Cross-Related by Kindred Fibonacci Fractions

Figure 7-3 combines the observations of Figures 7-1 and 7-2. The advancing waves are related by fractions of *alternate* Fibonacci numbers, representing $\phi^2$, and the corrective waves are related by fractions of *adjacent* Fibonacci numbers, representing $\phi$.

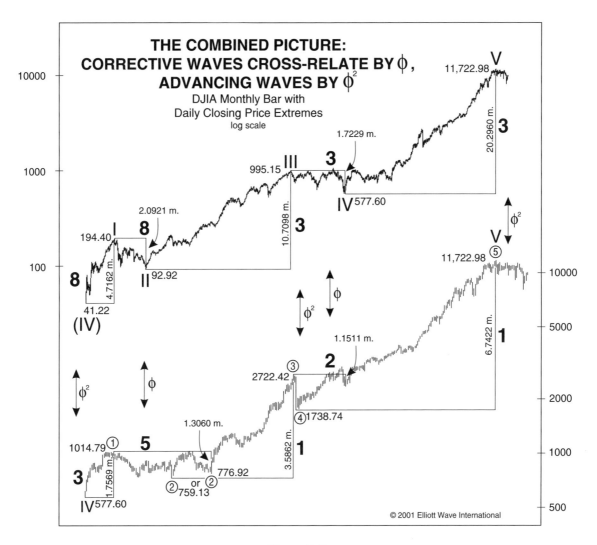

Figure 7-3

*Figure 7-4:*

## Waves ①-③ and ①-⑤ Are Cross-Related to Waves I-III and I-V, and Wave I Is Cross-Related to Wave (V)

Wave V from 1980 is related to wave (V) by .05430, which is very close to 3/55 (.05455) and exactly $(8/13)^6$ to four decimal places and nearly to five.

The main measuring units (waves one through three) for the Cycle and the Super-cycle are related by .1952, which is $\phi^4$, where $\phi$ = .6647, which is 2/3. (We should also recall from Figure 5-11 that in terms of multiples, ①-③ = I.)

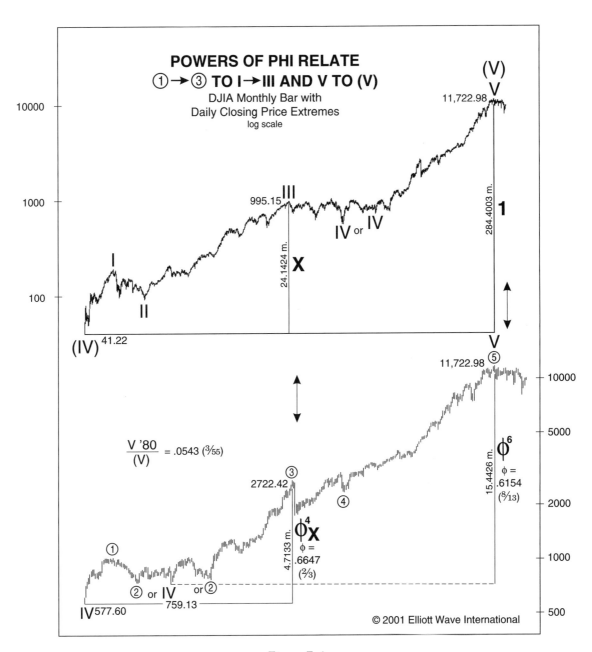

*Figure 7-4*

# Chapter 8

# TIME RELATIONSHIPS IN THE SUPERCYCLE

### Figure 8-1:

### Time Symmetry in Related Waves

Figure 8-1 shows four sets of symmetrical durations:
• Waves I and II each last **5** years.
• The 1987 crash separates Cycle wave V into two advances, each lasting a Fibonacci **13** years.
• The 1987 high of Primary wave ③ splits Cycle wave V into two sections, each lasting a Fibonacci **13** years.
• The two extended bull markets within the Supercycle each last 26 years. (This result occurs when measuring wave III to its speculative peak in 1968, when the secondary stock indexes such as the Value Line and the Amex topped out, on December 13 and December 16, respectively.)
• The 1966 high of Cycle wave III splits the entire Supercycle into two segments, each lasting a Fibonacci **34** years.

The 34-34-year experience in wave (V) mirrors the 13-13-year experience in wave V. In both cases, the peak of wave three divides the total duration into two equal parts, each a Fibonacci number of years long. 13/34 is a Fibonacci ratio. The 26-26-year experience in wave (V) somewhat mirrors the 13-13-year experience in wave V in being two advancing periods of equal duration separated by a correction. 13/26 is the Fibonacci ratio 1/2. The time ratio 1/1 also occurs, five times.

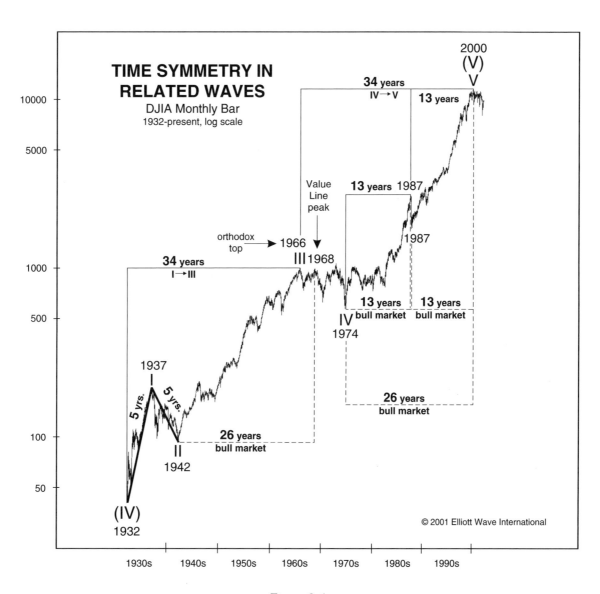

*Figure 8-1*

**Chapter 9**

# TIME RELATIONSHIPS IN CYCLE WAVE V

**Figure 9-1:**

**Alternate Fibonacci Durations for All Three Advances within Wave V, in Years**

Figure 9-1 shows that Cycle wave V unfolded primarily by way of three persistent upward movements. They lasted approximately 2 years, 5 years and 13 years. Notice that these durations reflect alternate numbers in the Fibonacci sequence: **2**, 3, **5**, 8, **13**. Thus, the relationships between the two sets of adjacent durations are 2/5 and 5/13, both of which are 1-ɸ. The time from the 1974 low to the 1987 high/low is also **13** years.

Three of the four periods shown lasted a Fibonacci number of years ± a small Fibonacci number of days. The first advance lasted **2** years minus **13** days; the second advance lasted **5** years plus **13** days; the total time of the combined period from the 1974 bottom to the 1987 bottom lasted **13** years minus **2** days. The third advance, from October 1987 to September 2000, lasted **13** years minus 43 days, the only difference that is not a Fibonacci number of days.

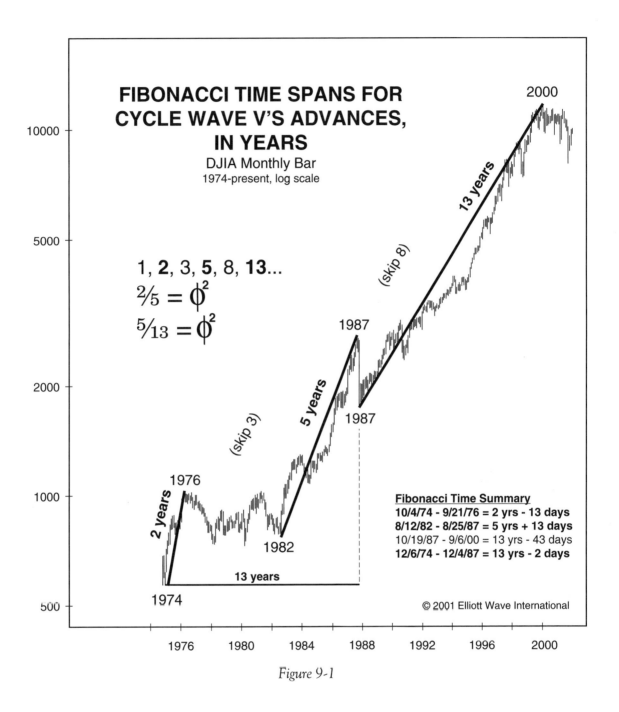

**FIBONACCI TIME SPANS FOR CYCLE WAVE V'S ADVANCES, IN YEARS**

DJIA Monthly Bar
1974-present, log scale

1, **2**, 3, **5**, 8, **13**...

$$2/5 = \phi^2$$
$$5/13 = \phi^2$$

**Fibonacci Time Summary**
10/4/74 - 9/21/76 = 2 yrs - 13 days
8/12/82 - 8/25/87 = 5 yrs + 13 days
10/19/87 - 9/6/00 = 13 yrs - 43 days
12/6/74 - 12/4/87 = 13 yrs - 2 days

© 2001 Elliott Wave International

Figure 9-1

***Figure 9-2:***

## Fibonacci Ratios Among All Three Advances within Wave V, in Days

The ratios between the precise number of *days* in the first two and final two advances are virtually identical. (See Figure 9-2.) The first advance, when measured from the S&P's low on 10/4/74 to 9/21/76, lasted 718 days. The second advance, from 8/12/82 to 8/25/87, lasted 1839 days. The final advance, from 10/19/87 to the S&P's second top (and possibly orthodox top; see Figure 4-8 in Chapter 4) on 9/6/00, lasted 4706 days. The ratio between the first two durations is **.3904**, and the ratio between the second two is **.3908**. The difference may be expressed as four days in the final advance or less than a single day in the first.

These two ratios, moreover, average .3906, which is $\phi^2$, where $\phi$ = **.6250**, which is **5/8**. Had the middle advance been a single day shorter, both ratios would be .3906 and have a perfect $(5/8)^2$ relationship. Again, intraday figures might produce this perfection. The ratio between the first and final advances is **.1526**, which is $\phi^4$, where $\phi$ = **.6250**, a perfect **5/8**. This remarkable set of time ratios appears to explain why the S&P held up until September 6, 2000.

In Figure 9-2, these three periods are labeled waves ①, ③, and ⑤ for easy reference. In the Dow, wave ③ may be labeled as beginning in 1982, although that labeling is less attractive in the S&P, which was outperforming the Dow at that time. The S&P's turning dates are employed in Figures 9-2 and 9-3 for the start and end of wave V.

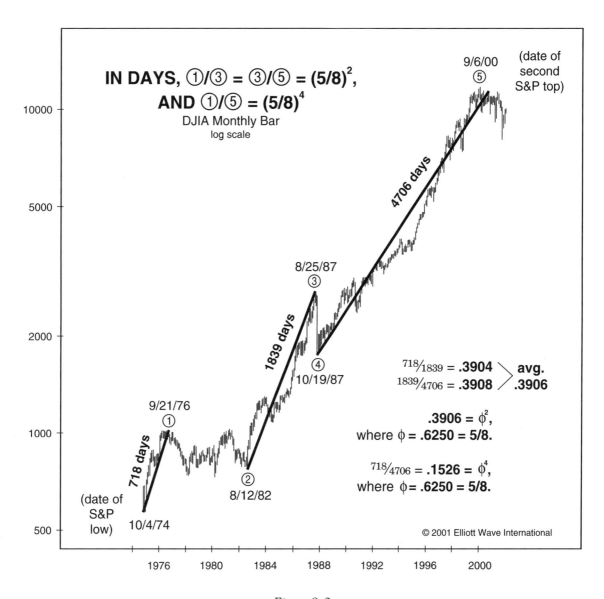

**IN DAYS, ①/③ = ③/⑤ = (5/8)², AND ①/⑤ = (5/8)⁴**

DJIA Monthly Bar
log scale

9/6/00
⑤

(date of second S&P top)

4706 days

8/25/87
③

1839 days

④
10/19/87

9/21/76
①

718 days

② 
8/12/82

(date of S&P low)
10/4/74

$^{718}/_{1839} = .3904$ ⟩ avg.
$^{1839}/_{4706} = .3908$ ⟩ .3906

**.3906 = φ²,**
where φ = .6250 = 5/8.

$^{718}/_{4706} = .1526 = φ⁴,$
where φ = .6250 = 5/8.

© 2001 Elliott Wave International

Figure 9-2

**Figure 9-3:**

The total duration from the 1974 low to the 1987 high is just 15 days short of being equal to the total duration of the advance from the 1987 low to the September 2000 top. Figure 9-3 also notes that the duration of the 1987 decline is a Fibonacci **55** days.

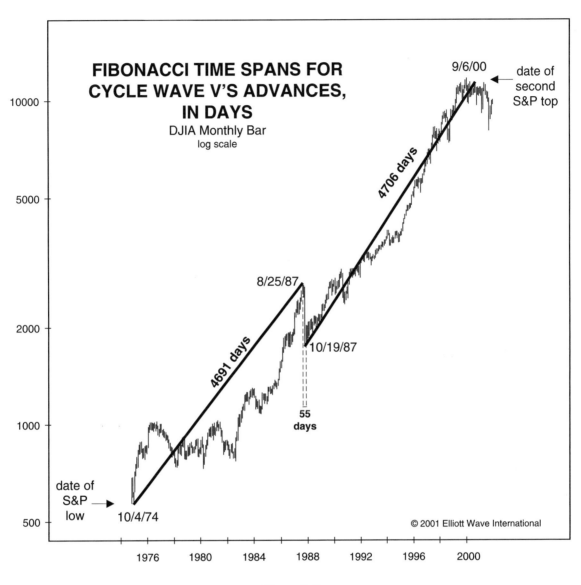

**FIBONACCI TIME SPANS FOR CYCLE WAVE V'S ADVANCES, IN DAYS**

DJIA Monthly Bar
log scale

9/6/00 — date of second S&P top

4706 days

8/25/87

4691 days

10/19/87

55 days

date of S&P low — 10/4/74

© 2001 Elliott Wave International

*Figure 9-3*

*Chapter 10*

# TIME CROSS-RELATIONSHIPS BETWEEN WAVES V AND (V)

Most relationships in this chapter are exactly or very close to Fibonacci number ratios. Most of them are precise to within 0 to 3 days in durations lasting years or decades.

*Figure 10-1:*

## Both the Entirety and the Components of Cycle Wave V Are in $\phi^2$ Relationship to the Entirety and Corresponding Components of Supercycle Wave (V), in Years

Figure 10-1 displays waves V and (V), which end simultaneously in the year 2000. It shows the number of years in the components, the entirety, and the segments produced by the midway split at the peak of each third wave and the Fibonacci split at the bottom of each fourth wave. In every one of these nine instances, the cross-relationship is $\phi^2$. The entire durations are 26 years and 68 years, and 26/68 = .382. The ratios involved in the cross-components are all Fibonacci-number ratios, in succession: 2/5, 3/8, 5/13, 8/21 and 13/34. The decimal expressions range from .375 to .400, approaching the limit ratio .382.

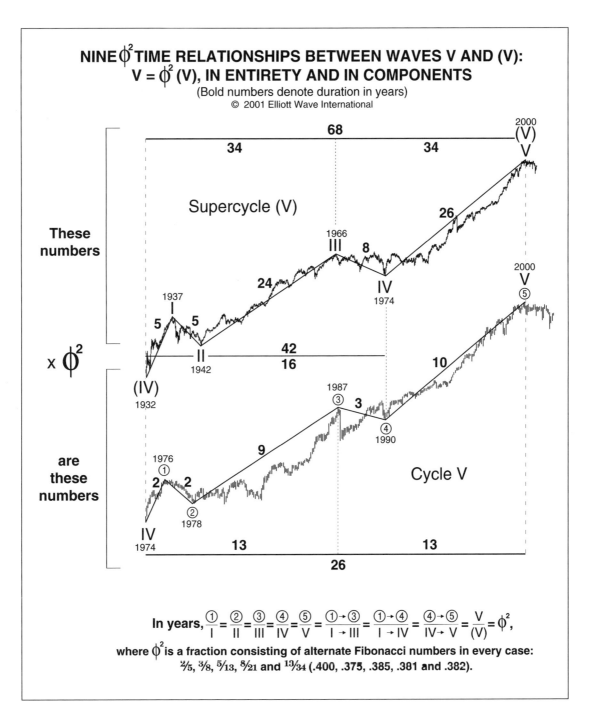

*Figure 10-1*

**Figures 10-2 and 10-3:**

## $\phi^2$ Cross-Relationships Between the Advances of Waves V and (V), Using an Exact Number of Days

The numbers of days in Primary waves ① and ③ within Cycle wave V have a $\phi^2$ relationship to their cousins within Supercycle wave (V), i.e., Cycle waves I and III. These ratios hold for both the S&P Composite index and the Dow Jones Industrial Average, as shown in Figures 10-2 and 10-3.

The .382 relationship maintains for the two fifth waves when marking the end of wave ④ in October 1990 and the orthodox top in September 2000, per Figure 4-8 in Chapter 4.

Using these dates, as you can see in Figure 10-2, all three advancing phases are in a $\phi^2$ relationship. In terms of the number of days involved in each segment, the differences from the limit ratio (.382) are only a Fibonacci 2 days, 5 days and 1 day, respectively, which are amazingly small differentials. In fact, all of the $\phi^2$ relationships in Figures 10-2 and 10-3 are between zero and only two days off from being exactly the limit ratio .382 or one of the Fibonacci-number ratios, **3/8, 5/13, 8/21** or **13/34**.

Recall that wave ③ has three acceptable starting points. Using the duration of 1839 days from 8/12/82 to 8/25/87 shown in Figure 9-2, ③/III in days (1839/8688) = **.2117**, which is $\phi^3$, where $\phi$ = .5960, which is approximately 3/5. The different starting and ending points, then, appear as if "trying" to form a web of Fibonacci relationships. This relationship is not shown in Figure 10-2 because it is too far from our range of acceptable tolerance.

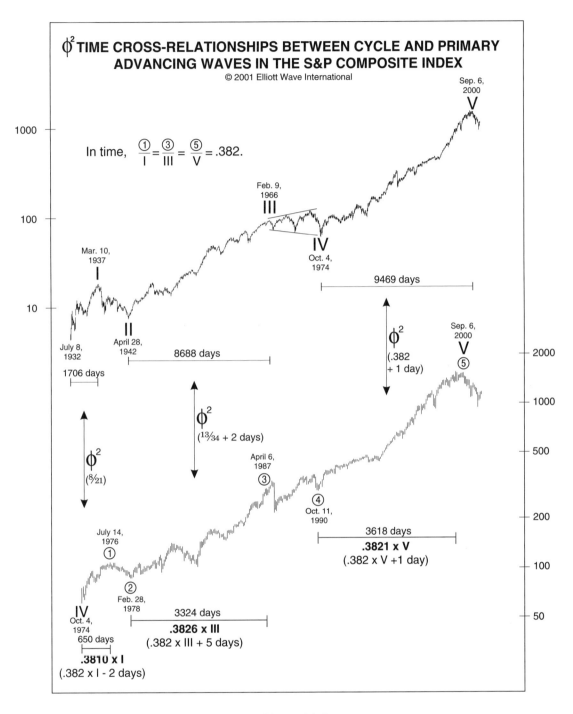

Figure 10-2

*Figure 10-3:*

## 3/8 and 1/2 Relationships When Starting Wave ⑤ from January 1991 and October 1987

During the 1990s, *The Elliott Wave Theorist* proposed an acceptable interpretation of Primary wave ④ as a contracting triangle from the 1987 high, ending on January 9, 1991, per Figure 4-7. Figure 10-3 displays the cross-relationship between fifth waves when measuring wave ⑤ from the end of the triangle pattern. This ratio between ⑤ and V on this basis is a nearly perfect **3/8**, yet another Fibonacci-number time ratio that is off only a single day.

If we maintain the starting point of Primary wave ⑤ in October 1987, we still find a Fibonacci relationship. From there, wave ⑤ to September 2000 is 1/2 the duration of Cycle wave V. The differential from perfection is only 3 days.

To sum up all three ⑤/V ratios, the starting points for wave ⑤ of 10/11/90, 1/9/91 and 10/19/87 produce ratios of **.382** (φ), **3/8** and **1/2**, and all of them are off by just a single day. Again, the different starting points produce a web of Fibonacci relationships.

Figure 10-3 displays a different cross-relationship for waves ①/I than that shown in Figure 10-2 by using the turn dates for the Dow rather than the S&P. The ratio in this case is .3845, which is four days off from .382 but *zero* days off from **5/13** (.3846).

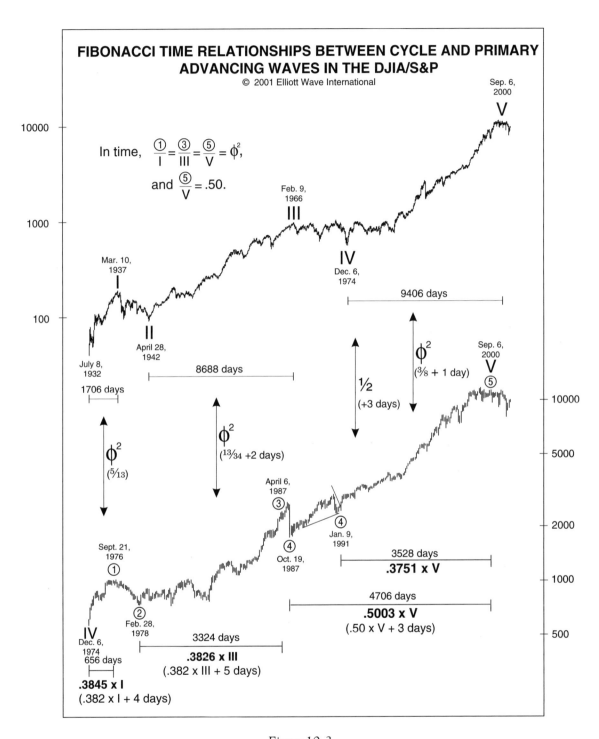

*Figure 10-3*

*Figure 10-4:*

## $\phi^2$ Cross-Relationships in the Durations of Corrective Waves

Just as the advancing sections of waves V and (V) are cross-related, so are the corrective waves. Primary wave ④ is related by $\phi^2$ to Cycle wave IV, with a differential from the limit ratio of only 2 days and from 13/34 of only 1 day.

Primary wave ② is likewise related by $\phi^2$ to Cycle wave II, but only if we date wave ② as beginning at March 24, 1976, when the persistent advance ended. This relationship is off from the limit ratio by 10 days and from 3/8 by 2 days.

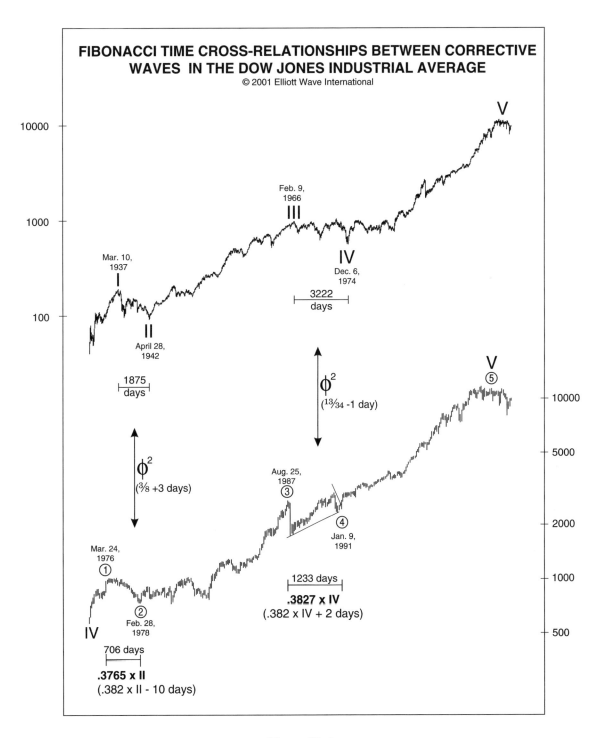

*Figure 10-4*

*Figures 10-5:*

## Waves V and (V) Are Cross-Related by $\phi^2$ on Each Side of the Split at Wave Three

The split at wave three divides each entire wave at almost exactly its halfway point, as we observed in Figures 2-4 and 2-7. As you can see in Figure 10-5, using the two available dates for the high of Primary wave ③, i.e., April 6 and August 25, 1987, the two halves of waves V and (V) are cross-related almost exactly by $\phi^2$. Depending upon which starting and ending dates we choose, we can express both the first and second half as .379 ±.001, making them nearly identical ratios, or as .3837 and .3765, which average to .380.

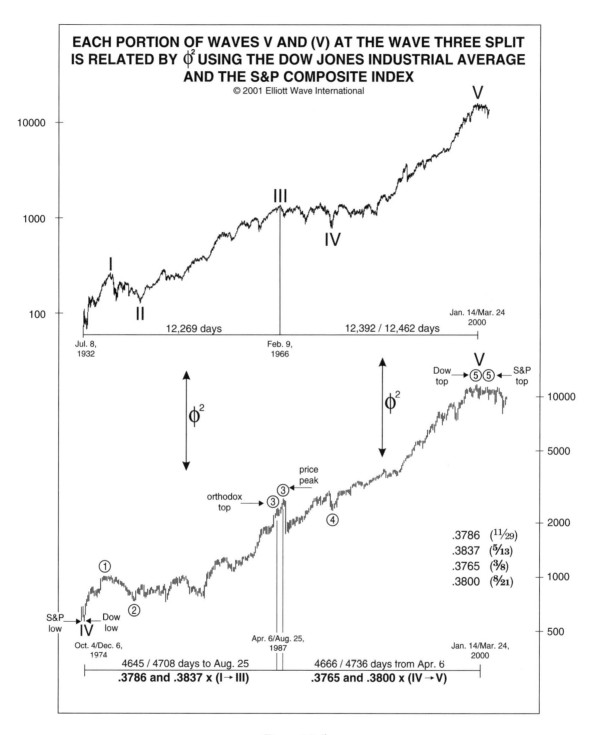

*Figure 10-5*

*Figure 10-6:*

## A Closer Relationship Using the S&P High of September 2000

Just as there are two tops for wave ③, there are two tops for wave V in the S&P, the second one occurring on September 6, 2000. As shown in Figure 10-6, for the ratios to work out at the first S&P high requires using the first top for wave ③. Figure 10-6 shows that using only the second top of wave ③, the ratios match at the second top of wave V. The two halves of waves V and (V) are cross-related by .3786 and .3770 respectively.

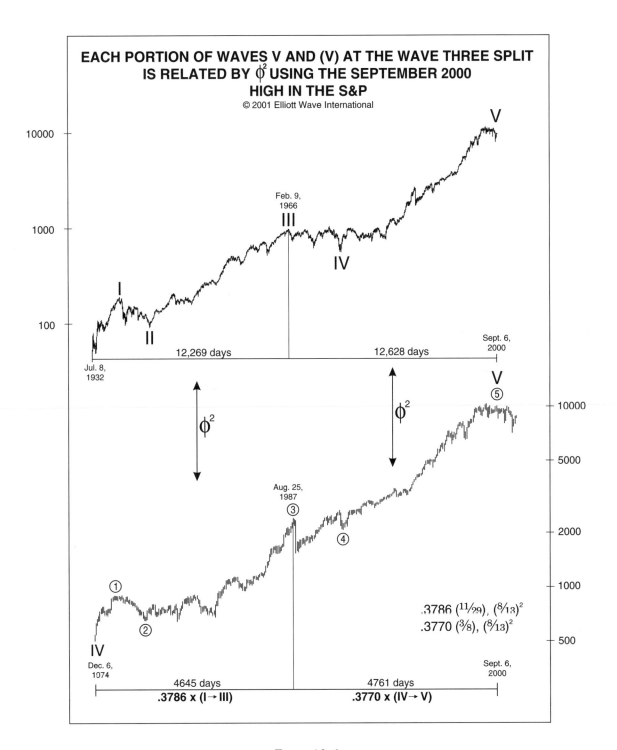

*Figure 10-6*

*Figure 10-7:*

## Wave Three Splits Waves V and (V) into Identical Proportion

The two halves of waves V and (V) are cross-related almost identically because the peak of wave three occurs very near the same point within each wave. This is very close to the halfway point, as shown earlier by the decimals within the notes on Figure 2-7. Figure 10-7 displays this excellent self-affinity. Chapter 11 will present and expand upon the similar significance of the end of wave four.

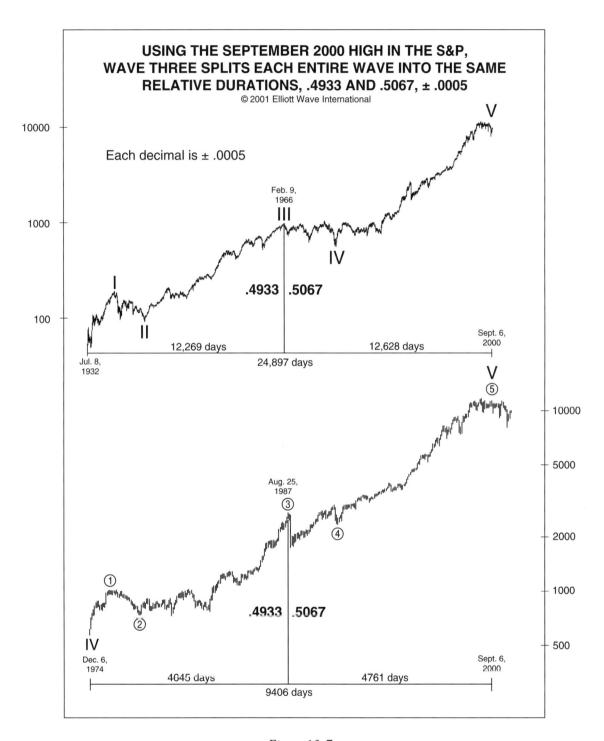

*Figure 10-7*

*Figure 10-8:*

## A $\phi^2$ Fibonacci Time Relationship between Waves V and (V)

Figure 10-8 shows three V/(V) time cross-relationships using the S&P's bottom on October 4, 1974 and the market's three tops in 2000. Generally speaking, Cycle wave V is extremely close to $\phi^2$ times the duration of Supercycle wave (V). The ratio to the Dow's peak on January 14, 2000 is .3744 and to the S&P's peak on March 24, 2000 is .3762, each of which is very close to **3/8** (.3750). Measuring to the final top on September 6, 2000, the ratio is .3803, which is approximately 8/21 (.38095).

Using the Dow's bottom on December 6, 1974, the ratios to the three successive tops are 9170/24,661, 9240/24,731 and 9406/24,897, which are .3718 (see Figure 2-8), .3736 (see Figure 11-2) and .3778, which is 11/29 and $(8/13)^2$ (see Figure 11-8). The last of these decimals is added to the listing for this figure in Table 4-L since it does not appear in this form elsewhere. It is interesting that the average of these three ratios is .3744, which is identical to the ratio when measuring wave V from October 1974 to January 2000 (see Figure 10-8). This is the closest of all the ratios to **3/8**, which appears to be the time-relationship "magnet" to which the components of these two waves are drawn. The average of all six ratios is .3757, and the mean is .3760.

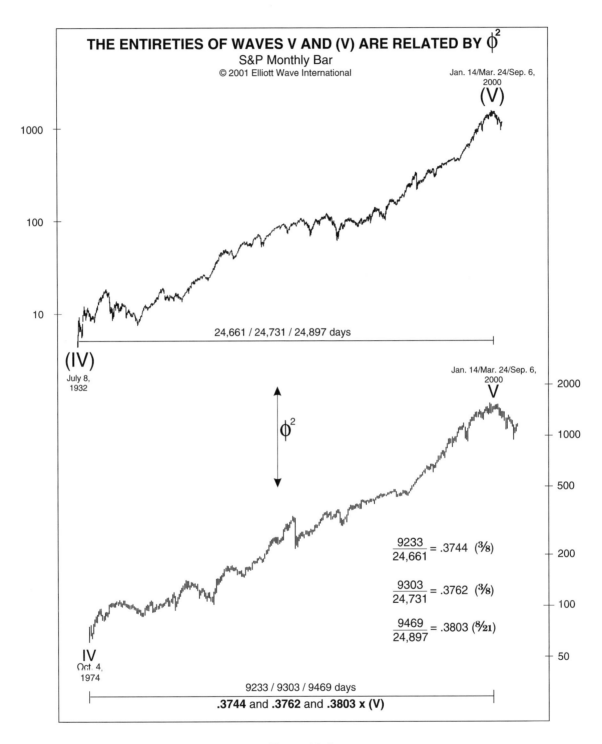

*Figure 10-8*

*Figure 10-9:*

## Fibonacci Relationships Between Various Waves ⑤ and V

Figure 10-9 combines observations accompanying Figures 10-2, 10-3, A-6 and B-7. It demonstrates how various expressions of wave ⑤ are related by Fibonacci fractions to various expressions of wave V.

The cited relationship to length A is fudged, as the ending dates of the two durations are different. It is included in order to show a fifth-wave relationship using 1982 as the end of wave IV, but the contrivance required is the reason it is not cited in Figure A-6. The rest of the ratios use identical ending dates.

While this figure could have been laid out like Figures 10-2 and 10-3, the relationships are shown on a single data series to give a different visual perspective on these cross-relationships.

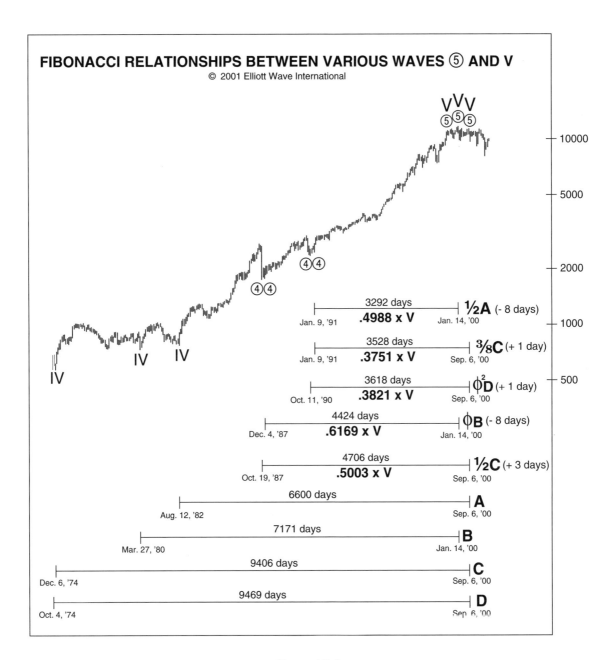

*Figure 10-9*

**Chapter 11**

# Elaboration on a Special Case:
# Wave Four and the Golden Section

*Figure 11-1:*

### Fifth Waves at Three Consecutive Degrees Form a Hierarchy

As displayed in Figure 11-1, Primary wave ⑤ from 1990 has the same time relationship to its parent, Cycle wave V as Cycle wave V has to its parent, Supercycle wave (V). The durations are 10 years, 26 years and 68 years. Thus, all three fifth waves, terminating simultaneously, are related by the Fibonacci numbers **5**, **13** and **34**, so that ⑤/V = V/(V) = $\phi^2$.

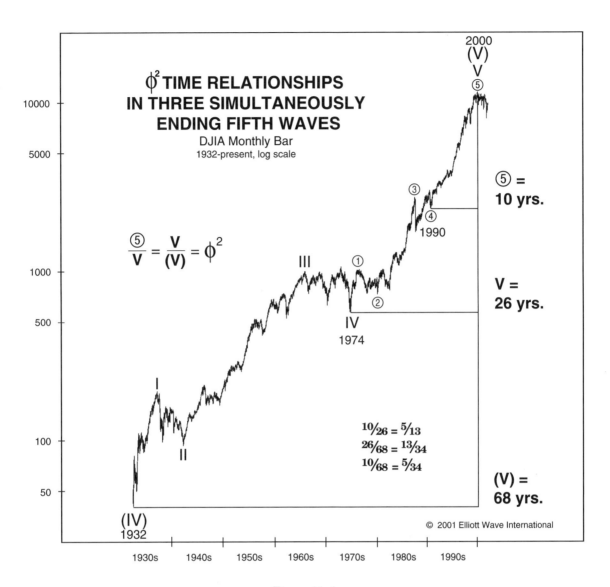

$\phi^2$ TIME RELATIONSHIPS
IN THREE SIMULTANEOUSLY
ENDING FIFTH WAVES

DJIA Monthly Bar
1932-present, log scale

$$\frac{\text{⑤}}{\text{V}} = \frac{\text{V}}{\text{(V)}} = \phi^2$$

⑤ =
10 yrs.

V =
26 yrs.

(V) =
68 yrs.

$$\frac{10}{26} = \frac{5}{13}$$
$$\frac{26}{68} = \frac{13}{34}$$
$$\frac{10}{68} = \frac{5}{34}$$

© 2001 Elliott Wave International

*Figure 11-1*

***Figure 11-2:***

## Wave Four Divides the Total Duration in Days Exactly into a .6264/.3736 Proportion in Waves V and (V)

Recall that the three fourth-wave time ratios in Figure 2-8, while quite close to each other in terms of days, are not quite the same. The only way that the ratios pertaining to waves V and (V) (the top two graphs in that figure) could be identical would be for the Dow to have continued to rise after the peak of January 14, 2000. In fact, the primary blue-chip average, the S&P 500 Composite Index, did top later, by 70 days, on March 24, 2000. By continuing to rise until that date, the stock market created the following wave relationships:

- *Within wave V:* Wave ④ ends at 5788 days out of 9240 days, at the **.6264** division point.
- *Within wave (V):* Wave IV ends at 15,491 days out of 24,731 days, at the **.6264** division point.

These two ratios are identical! In fact, they are nearly identical to five decimal places, at .62641 and .62642, respectively. It follows that the corresponding fifth waves each last the same percentage of the total time as well:

- *Within wave V:* Wave ⑤ lasts 3452 days out of 9240 days, or **.3736** of the total.
- *Within wave (V):* Wave V lasts 9240 days out of 24,731 days, or **.3736** of the total.

Thus, in Cycle wave V and again in the entire Supercycle, the split at wave four divides the entire wave exactly at a **.6264/.3736** time division in days when using the date for the low of the Dow in 1974 and the date of the high for the S&P in 2000. (See Figure 11-2.) In other words, once wave ④ ended in October 1990, the market had to rise until exactly March 24, 2000 in order for both waves ⑤ and V, which by definition end simultaneously, to end up having the same time relationship to their corresponding waves one through four. That's exactly what it did. To appreciate the nearness of these numbers, realize that a single day's difference within these decade-long advances would have disallowed identical ratios to four decimal places. In other words, no other date for the final high could have made the ratios closer.

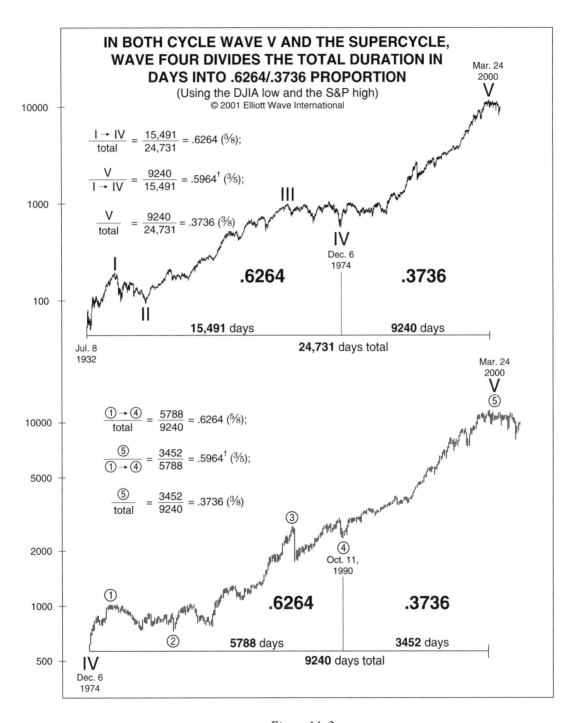

*Figure 11-2*

*Figure 11-3:*

## Waves V and (V) are Time Cross-Related Exactly by .3736 ($\phi^2$) on Each Side of the Split at Wave Four

Figure 11-3 shows a remarkable additional fact. Because wave ⑤ is the simultaneously ending fifth-wave component of wave V, each of the two sections of waves V and (V) are also *cross*-related in time exactly by the same ratio, **.3736** ($\phi^2$). In terms of duration in days, not only does ⑤/**V** = **V/(V)** = **.3736** but also ①-④/**I-IV** = **.3736**. In other words, the same ratio that governs each fifth wave as it relates to the total structure also governs the components of wave V on either side of wave ④ as they relate to the corresponding components of wave (V) on either side of wave IV.

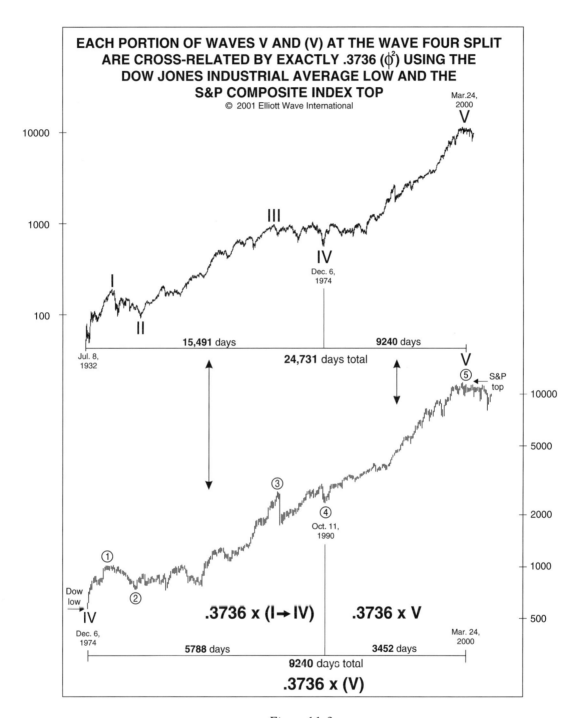

*Figure 11-3*

## *Figure 11-4:*

## Identical Relationships in Terms of Days Shown on One Data Series

Figure 11-4 shows the three .3736 relationships on one data series for a different perspective. Note also that this decimal is almost exactly 11/18, so that the two sets of adjacent waves are related by $(11/18)^2$ and the alternate waves, ⑤ and (V), are related by $(11/18)^4$.

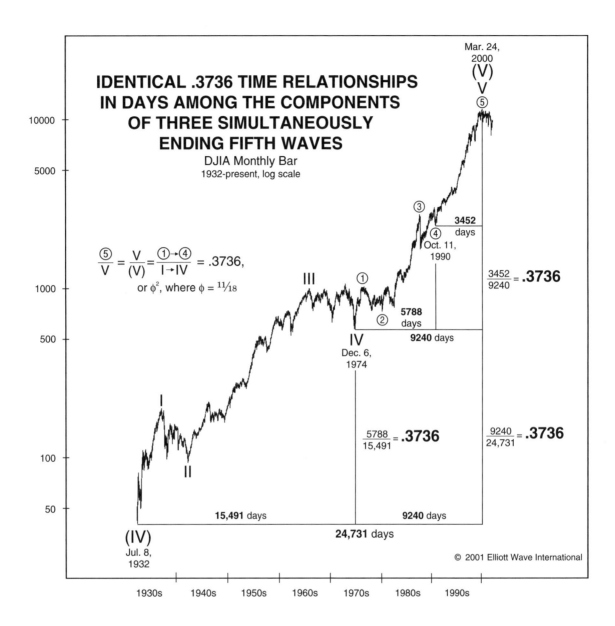

IDENTICAL .3736 TIME RELATIONSHIPS
IN DAYS AMONG THE COMPONENTS
OF THREE SIMULTANEOUSLY
ENDING FIFTH WAVES
DJIA Monthly Bar
1932-present, log scale

$$\frac{⑤}{V} = \frac{V}{(V)} = \frac{①→④}{I→IV} = .3736,$$

or $\phi^2$, where $\phi = {}^{11}\!/_{18}$

$$\frac{3452}{9240} = .3736$$

$$\frac{5788}{15,491} = .3736 \qquad \frac{9240}{24,731} = .3736$$

*Figure 11-4*

*Figure 11-5:*

## A Fibonacci 5/3 Fraction in Days

Each portion of the time division depicted in Figure 11-2 relates to the others approximately by a Fibonacci number ratio. The duration up to the low of wave four is .6264 (close to **5/8**) of the total duration, the duration of wave five is .5964 (close to **3/5**) of the duration up to the low of wave four, and the duration of wave five is .3736 (close to **3/8**) of the total duration.

Figure 11-5 shows how Fibonacci numbers represent the three durations within each of these waves. The shared time factor is 1155 days for wave V and 3091.375 days for wave (V), so that each entire duration is 8 times its time factor and the sections are approximately 3 and 5 times that factor.

Even the "approximately" is interesting and probably instructive. The difference from a perfect ratio within wave V is a Fibonacci **13** days. The first section is 13 days "too long," and wave ⑤ is 13 days "short," which means had the wave ④ low occurred 13 days later, the split would have been exactly at the 3/5 point. The difference from a perfect ratio in the Supercycle is a Fibonacci **34** days, which means had the wave IV low occurred 34 days later, the split would have occurred exactly at the 3/5 point.

Now get this. The ratio between 13 and 34 is $\phi^2$, which is the same as the ratio between the two entire durations. Therefore, had wave IV ended 34 days later (on January 9, 1975) to make the time split of the Supercycle form perfect 3/5, 3/8 and 5/8 ratios among the durations of its sections, then the low of wave ④ would already be in exactly the right place to divide the resulting total duration of wave V so as to produce the same perfect ratios!

Having done many exercises such as this, I have found a substantial number of times when a long term Fibonacci relationship is nearly perfect yet offset by some small Fibonacci component. It reminds me of the tiny mutations in DNA that allow species to experiment repeatedly with modicums of diversity. I said in *The Wave Principle of Human Social Behavior* that I do not believe DNA mutations to be random but rather governed by Fibonacci; the same appears to be true of these slight "mutations" of perfect Fibonacci ratios in the stock market.

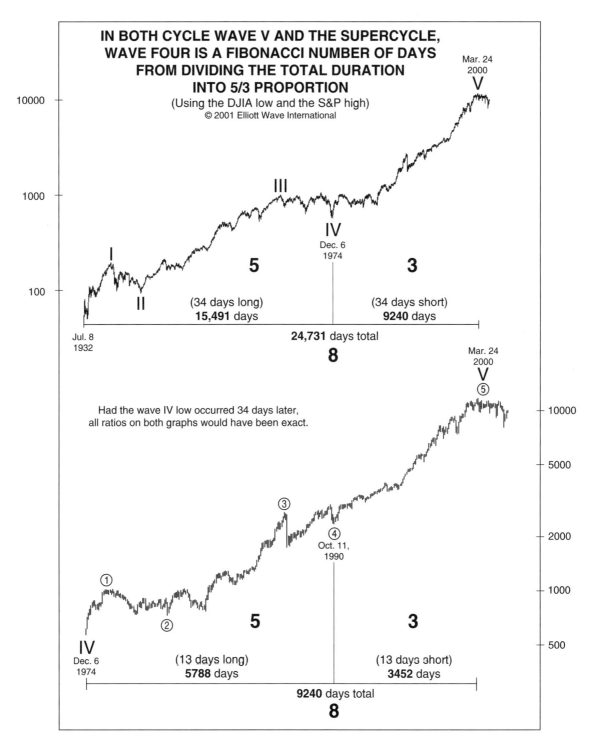

Figure 11-5

## *Figure 11-6:*

## A Fibonacci Progression

Now for the next step. If each wave five is related to the preceding section by a Fibonacci ratio, and if the smaller wave is the fifth-wave component of the larger wave, then all five durations are related by Fibonacci, in sequence! Figure 11-6 shows that from wave ⑤ of V to wave (V) of Ⅲ, all the sections form a Fibonacci progression of durations: 3, 5, 8, 13 and 21.

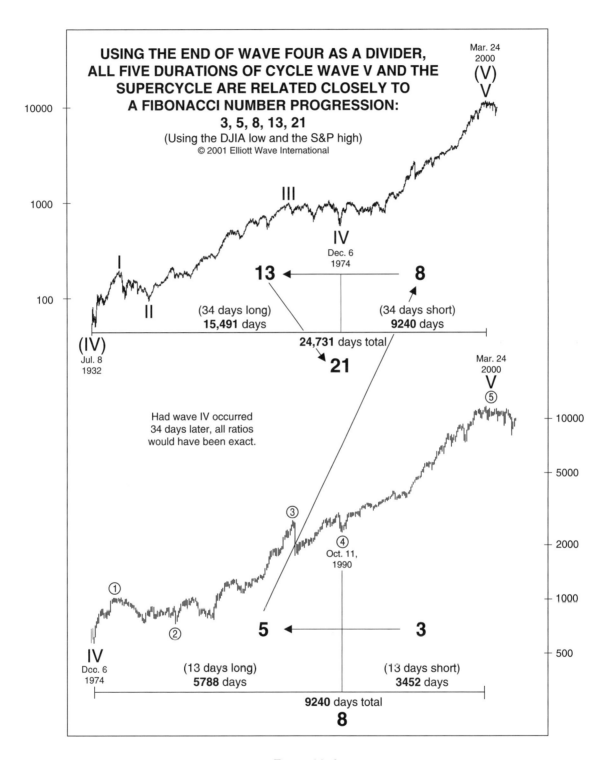

*Figure 11-6*

## *Figure 11-7:*

## The Fibonacci-Number Relationships Among Wave Components on One Data Series

Figure 11-7 shows the relationships among these wave components on one data series. The duration of each segment is 1171 days (±21 days) times a Fibonacci number from 3 to 21, in sequence.

Recall from Figures 11-5 and 11-6 that the differentials from ideal durations are **13** and **34** days. The maximum differential from the shared factor of 1171 days is **21** days (which appears in the 3x and 13x sections). So the differentials from ideal durations that the market employs in this array are 13, 21 and 34 days, which are consecutive Fibonacci numbers.

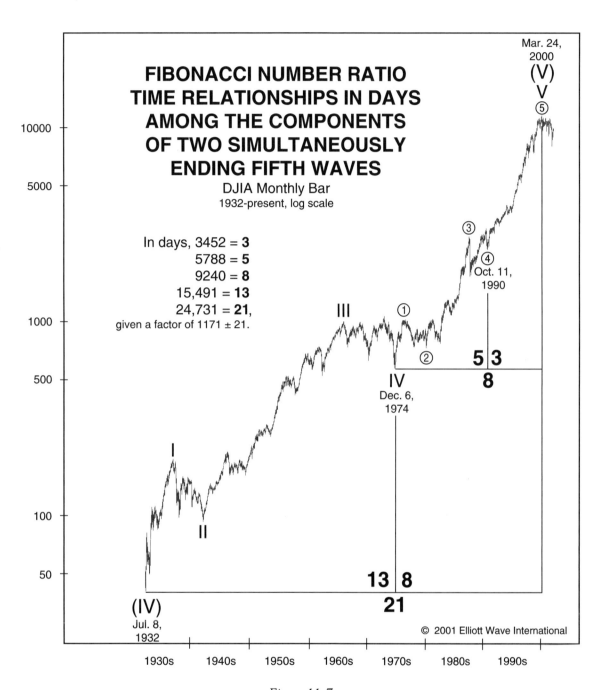

**FIBONACCI NUMBER RATIO TIME RELATIONSHIPS IN DAYS AMONG THE COMPONENTS OF TWO SIMULTANEOUSLY ENDING FIFTH WAVES**

DJIA Monthly Bar
1932-present, log scale

In days, 3452 = **3**
5788 = **5**
9240 = **8**
15,491 = **13**
24,731 = **21**,
given a factor of 1171 ± 21.

Mar. 24, 2000
(V)
V
⑤

③
④
Oct. 11, 1990

III
①

②
IV
Dec. 6, 1974

**5** **3**
**8**

**13** **8**
**21**

I
II

(IV)
Jul. 8, 1932

© 2001 Elliott Wave International

1930s    1940s    1950s    1960s    1970s    1980s    1990s

*Figure 11-7*

*Figure 11-8:*

## Edging Closer to a .618 Time Ratio

As shown in Figure 11-2, the ratios are identical on March 24, 2000, but they are not the ideal limit ratios, .618 and .382. Did the stock market do anything important around the time that would have made either of the waves end at that ratio? Well, the S&P held up until September 6, 2000, making a slightly lower peak on that date that can be labeled the "orthodox top," the details of which are shown in Figure 4-8. Using that date, we have the following relationship, as illustrated in Figure 11-8:

- *Within wave* V: Wave ④ ends at 5788 days out of 9406 days, at the **.6154** division point, which is exactly **8/13**.
- *Within wave* (V): Wave IV ends at 15,491 days out of 24,897 days, at the **.6222** division point, which is 58 days short of **5/8**.

The average of these two ratios is **.6188**.

To conclude, the S&P first topped precisely so as to make the two internal wave ratios identical. Then it held up long enough to make the two ratios bracket the number .618, making each one of them nearly as close to .618 as possible.

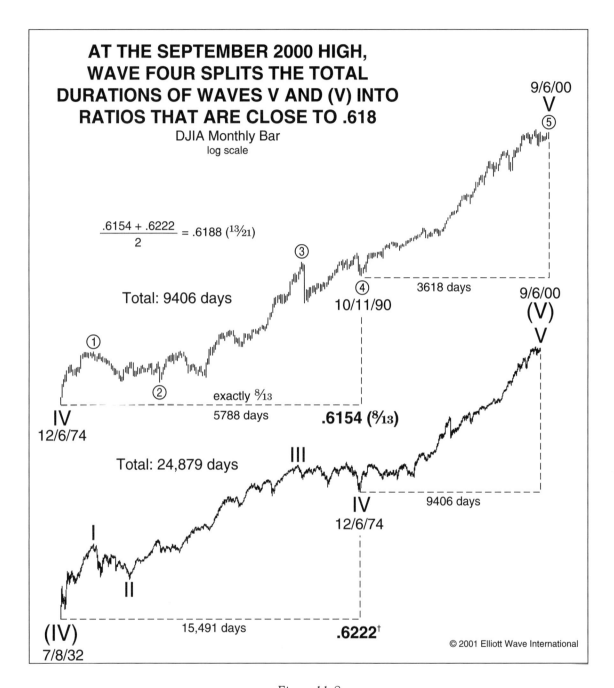

**AT THE SEPTEMBER 2000 HIGH,
WAVE FOUR SPLITS THE TOTAL
DURATIONS OF WAVES V AND (V) INTO
RATIOS THAT ARE CLOSE TO .618**

DJIA Monthly Bar
log scale

$$\frac{.6154 + .6222}{2} = .6188 \ (^{13}\!/_{21})$$

Total: 9406 days

9/6/00
V
⑤

3618 days     9/6/00
(V)
V

① ③ ④
10/11/90

② exactly ⁸⁄₁₃
5788 days
.6154 (⁸⁄₁₃)

IV
12/6/74

Total: 24,879 days

III

IV
12/6/74

9406 days

I

II

(IV)          15,491 days          .6222†
7/8/32

© 2001 Elliott Wave International

*Figure 11-8*

*Figure 11-9:*

## A Closer Ratio in the S&P

As already explored in Figure 10-2 from a different perspective, the S&P's turning point dates allow the duration of wave ⑤ to be a nearly perfect .382 as long as that of wave V, which means that the preceding wave structure lasts almost exactly .618 as long. As Figure 11-9 shows, the low of wave ④ divides the entire rise at the **.6179** point. Wave ⑤ ended just *two days* after the time that would have provided the closest possible match to the ideal limit ratio of .618034. Alternatively, we can say that had the daily closing low for wave ④ occurred a single day later, on October 12, 1990, the split would have been precise. Again, intraday figures may have made this relationship exact. Along with Figure 11-2, this graph is another hint that these time relationships are actually occurring with precision, whether our data is always sufficient to reveal that fact or not.

Using these dates also brings the components of wave (V) closer to phi, with the division coming at the **.6197** point, as also shown in Figure 11-9. The only way for the Supercycle to have achieved a .618 ratio would have been for the market to hold up for another 66 days, but doing so would have damaged the .618 ratio in Cycle wave V. The dividing date in this case is 16 days off from the Fibonacci fraction **13/21**. Remarkably often, such periods are numbers that are the difference between two Fibonacci numbers (in this case, 21 minus 5), as if the market were "spiraling" into the final date.

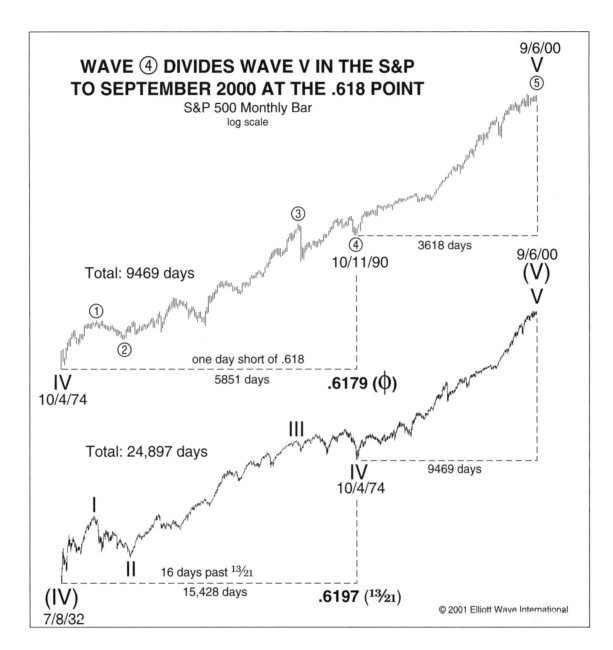

Figure 11-9

*Figure 11-10:*

## Wave Four as an Identical Divider of Both Price and Time

To appreciate fully the identical positioning of the end of wave four in these two waves, refer back to Figure 2-11 and recall that the two fourth wave endpoints divide both waves at almost exactly the same logarithmic *price* point. *So the end of wave four is a perfectly identical marker in time and a nearly identical marker in price for these two waves*, which terminate simultaneously. Figure 11-10 consolidates these observations.

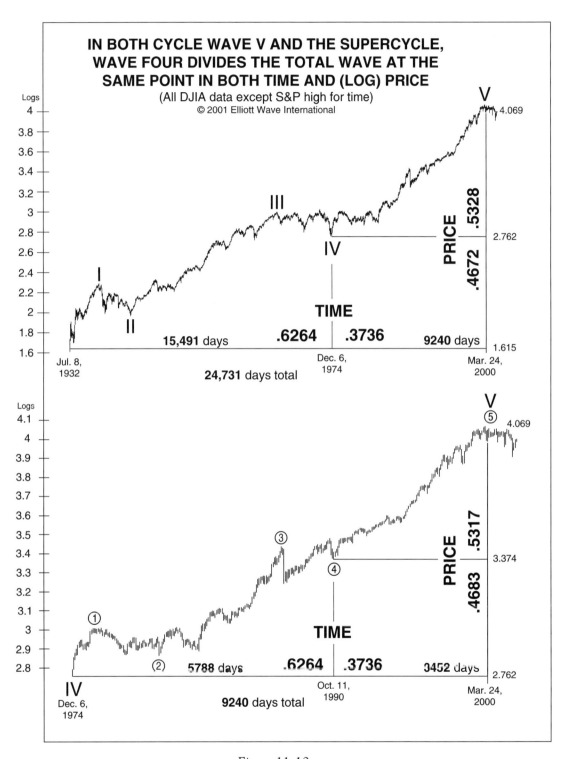

*Figure 11-10*

## *Figure 11-11:*

## The Wave Four Time and Price Divisions on One Data Series

Figure 11-11 displays the wave four time and price divisions on one data series to show how they fit together.

Thus, we may have a new Elliott wave guideline, which is that the end of wave four can be a *time and price divider* that identically subdivides an impulse wave and its same-number component.

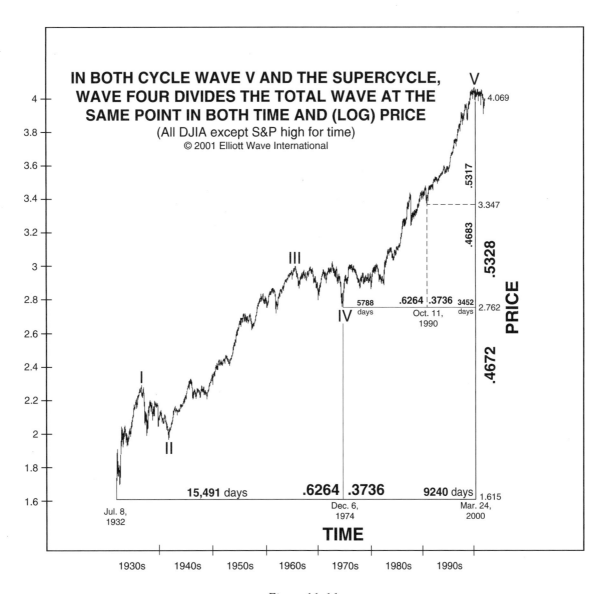

Figure 11-11

*Figure 11-12:*

## Fibonacci Fractions in Price and Time

As noted in Figure 11-2, the time ratio that pertains to the period prior to the start of each fifth wave relative to the whole is .6264, which is close to .625, which is **5/8**. We can say, then, that the *time preceding the start of wave* ⑤ is **5/8** of the *entire time of wave* V, and the *time preceding the start of wave* V is **5/8** of the *entire time of wave* (V). Therefore, the time ratio between each component is **3/5**, as shown in Figure 11-12. Both 5/8 and 3/5, of course, are expressions of phi.

Recall that Figure 6-5 shows that we have a similar situation in terms of price. The price multiple of wave V is **5/8** of the price multiple of the advance preceding wave V (i.e., up to the top of wave III). As noted with Figure 5-1, this calculation is so close that it is off by a negligible 0.03 in the Dow for an advance that lasted most of the 20th century. The ratio projects a price of 11,722.95, and the actual closing high was 11,722.98. In this case, the identical relationship does not hold true at one lesser degree, but the *inverse* does. The net price multiple of waves ①-③ is **5/8** of the price multiple of wave ⑤. As noted with Figure 6-4, this calculation is off by only 6.46 Dow points at the high.

Figure 11-12 shows these observations combined. These results may reveal another guideline, which is that at least in extended fifth waves within larger fifth waves, wave five is related by φ in *price* to the net gain up to a *start* of wave four, while it is simultaneously related by φ in *time* to the net duration up to an *end* of wave four.

While usually these are single points, Figure 11-12 uses two termination points for wave IV. While this duality may mar what would otherwise be a perfect picture were Figure 11-12 to be viewed as a physical object, the concert among valid turning points identified in advance strictly by wave form suggests at least as interesting a feat in the market's having taken both major turning points into account when forming this simple yet elegant web of Fibonacci price and time relationships. It may not be too much to say that Figures 2-12 and 11-12 combine to suggest hidden quantitative governors of the robust quasi-Euclidean geometry of wave forms.

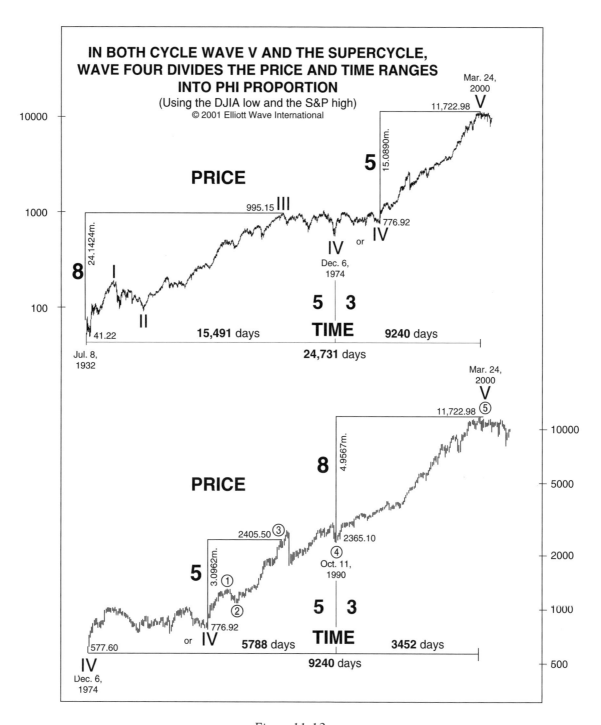

*Figure 11-12*

*Figure 11-13:*

## The Fibonacci Fractions on a Single Data Series

Figure 11-13 shows the Fibonacci numbers representing the four time and price relationships on one graph.

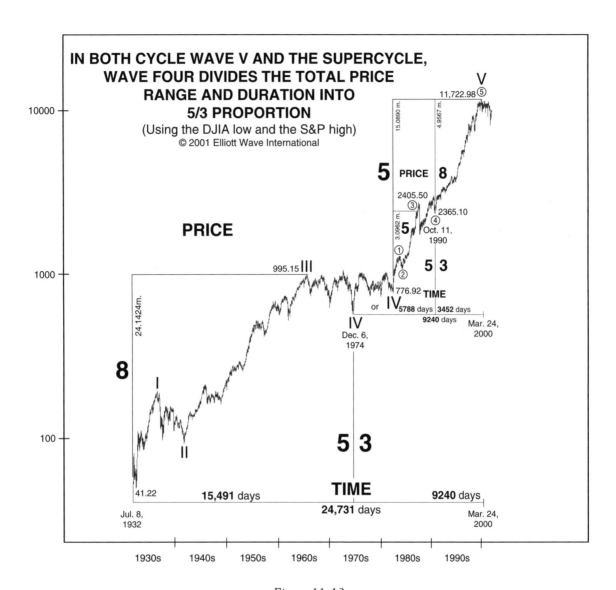

*Figure 11-13*

# Chapter 12

# *ADDITIONAL OBSERVATIONS*

## *Figure 12-1:*

### Identical Rates of Change among Three Affiliated Elliott Waves

As mentioned in Chapter 1, wave V in the Dow from December 1974 to January 2000 traveled very nearly the same net rate of non-compounded percentage gain over time as did wave V of the 1920s. There is a lot more to say on this subject. If we use the duration for the S&P instead of the Dow, the equality is even closer.

The gain of the recent wave V in the Dow is 1929.60%, and the gain of wave V from the 1920s (hereafter designated V20s) is 596.51%, for a gain ratio between them of **3.2348**. From the Dow's low on December 6, 1974 to its high on January 14, 2000, wave V spans 9170 days, and the duration of wave V20s is 2932 days. The duration ratio between them is **3.1276**, which is very nearly the same as the gain ratio. Using the S&P's low on October 4, 1974 to the S&P's orthodox top on September 6, 2000, wave V spans 9469 days. The duration ratio on this basis is **3.2295**. *To two decimal places, then, we can say that the gain and duration ratios for these two waves are the same, at* **3.23**. Had wave V in the S&P ended 15 days later, the ratios would have been identical. In other words, the two advances have almost exactly *the same net rate of non-compounded percentage change* (hereafter designated the "speed").

Wave V is affiliated not only with its cousin, wave V20s, but also to wave I from 1932 to 1937, the wave against which it relates for targeting purposes (see Chapter 3). Let's see if their affinity extends to their net rates of change.

The gain of wave V is 1929.60%, and the gain of wave I is 371.62%, for a gain ratio of **5.1924**. From the Dow's low on December 6, 1974 to its high on January 14, 2000, wave V spans 9170 days. Wave I spans 1706 days, for a duration ratio of **5.3751**. These ratios are quite close to each other, at **5.3 + or – 0.1**. In other words, these two advances also have nearly the same speed, which means that *all three of these advances have nearly the same net speed*.

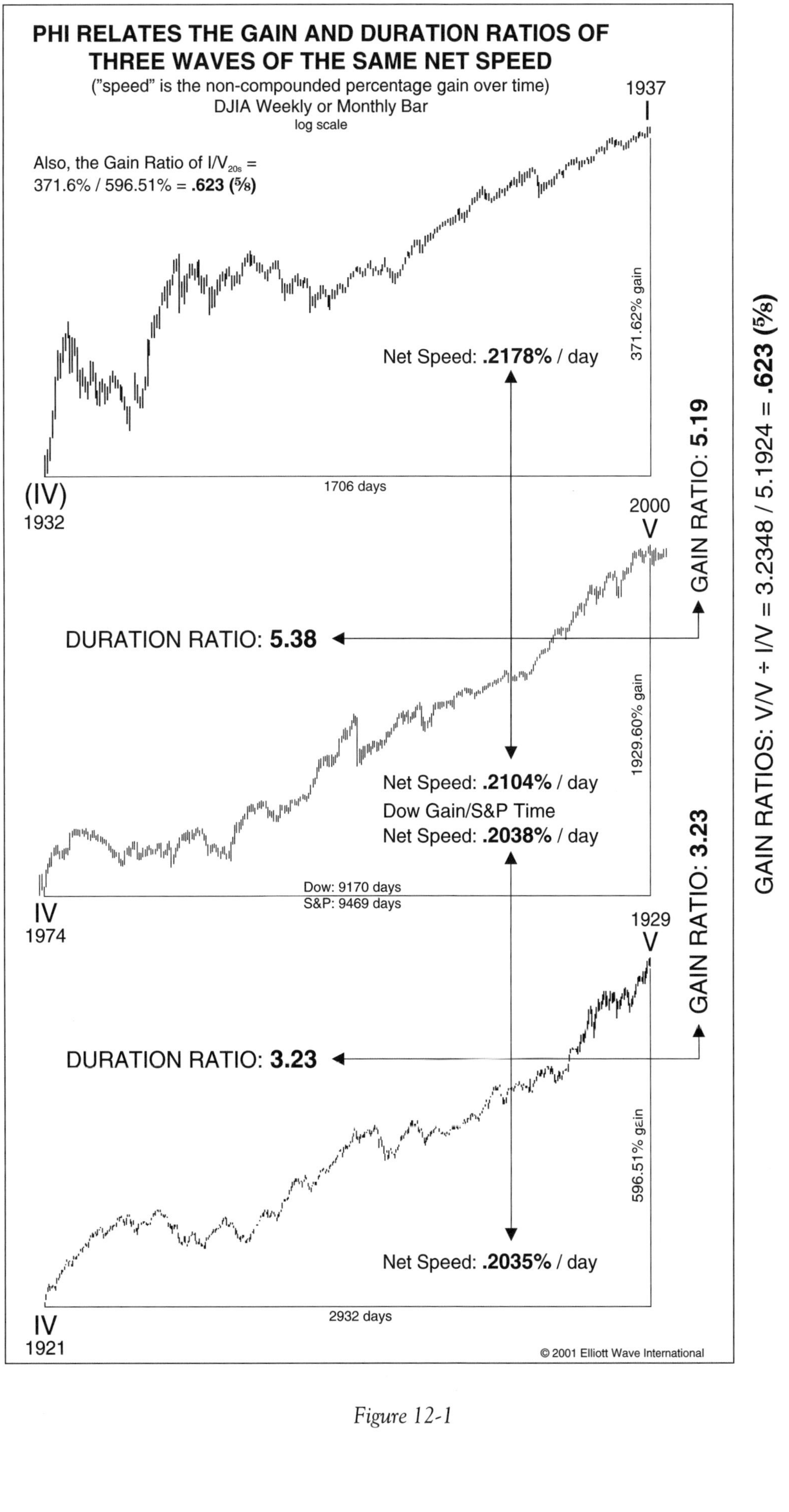

# PHI RELATES THE GAIN AND DURATION RATIOS OF THREE WAVES OF THE SAME NET SPEED

("speed" is the non-compounded percentage gain over time)
DJIA Weekly or Monthly Bar
log scale

Also, the Gain Ratio of I/V$_{20s}$ =
371.6% / 596.51% = **.623** (⅝)

1937
I

371.62% gain

Net Speed: **.2178%** / day

1706 days

(IV)
1932

DURATION RATIOS: V/V ÷ I/V = 3.2295 / 5.3751 = **.601** (⅗)

GAIN RATIOS: V/V ÷ I/V = 3.2348 / 5.1924 = **.623** (⅝)

GAIN RATIO: **5.19**

2000
V

DURATION RATIO: **5.38**

1929.60% gain

Net Speed: **.2104%** / day
Dow Gain/S&P Time
Net Speed: **.2038%** / day

Dow: 9170 days
S&P: 9469 days

IV
1974

1929
V

GAIN RATIO: **3.23**

DURATION RATIO: **3.23**

596.51% gain

Net Speed: **.2035%** / day

2932 days

IV
1921

© 2001 Elliott Wave International

*Figure 12-1*

Wave V in the Dow gained on average **.20378%** per day using the S&P's turning point dates and **2.1043%** per day using the Dow's turning point dates. Wave V20s gained on average .20345% per day, and wave I gained on average .21783% per day. Wave V, by sporting two sets of durations, thereby approaches each of the other waves' rates of change more precisely. Thus, while these three bull markets take different routes to get to their destinations, and while those destinations in price and time are different, they all travel at the same net speed (as defined above).

Turn back to Figure 1-3 and observe that the fifth wave that took place in the first half of the 1830s and the first wave that took place in the first half of the 1860s both appear to have roughly the same rate of change as these three bull markets. I have not investigated the data because one has to stop somewhere, and this is as far as I care to go along this path. (For a bit more on wave relationships in percentage terms, see Appendix C.)

## Fibonacci Relationships

These identical speeds would be interesting enough by themselves, but it is even more striking that Fibonacci relationships connect all three waves.

The gain ratio of V/V20s to that of V/I is 3.2348/5.1924 = **.623 (5/8)**.

The duration ratio of $V_{S\&P}$/V20s to that of $V_{Dow}$/I is 3.2295/5.3751 = **.601 (3/5)**. (Using $V_{Dow}$/V20s, the ratio is 3.1276/5.3751 = .5819.)

Combined, wave V's median price-and-time multiple of wave I (**3.232**) and its price-and-time multiple of wave V20s (**5.284**) are related by 3.232/5.284 = **.612**.

This result suggests that the bull markets of the 1920s and 1930s are also related by Fibonacci. The percentage gains of the 1930s and the 1920s are 371.6% and 596.51%, which are related by **.6230**, which is 0.32 percent from **5/8** (a ratio that features prominently in Chapters 5 through 11). In terms of time, the numbers of days in these waves are 1706 and 2932, which are related by 0.5818, which is not a Fibonacci number ratio but approximately 4/7 (.5714). The key observations in this section are illustrated in Figure 12-1.

## A Hint That Fibonacci Relationships Govern All the Waves

I could be satisfied at this point having shown that wave V20s and wave I are related to wave V, since they had pre-established affiliations to each other, the first by sharing number and degree and the second in typically forming a Fibonacci price relationship. Indeed, in terms of net speed, all three waves are overall the same event, while their differences of time and gain are expressed by Fibonacci ratios.

There is little question in my mind that if time allowed, we would find that many of the various gain and duration ratios among other related waves are also in Fibonacci proportion. To demonstrate this potential, let's examine just one more wave.

Wave III, from 1942 to 1966, gained 970.98% in 8688 days, which on average is .11176% per day (again, from the starting point, not compounded). This is just over half the speed of — and therefore much slower than — the three bull markets discussed above (waves I, V and V$_{20s}$).

The gain ratio between wave V and wave III is 1929.60%/970.98% = **1.9873**. As it happens, this V/III gain ratio is in Fibonacci relationship both to the V/V$_{20s}$ gain ratio and to the V/I gain ratio:

V/III vs. V/V$_{20s}$ is 1.9873/3.2348 = **.6144**

V/III vs. V/I is 1.9873/5.1924 = **.3827**.

These are nearly perfect expressions of the first two Fibonacci limit ratios. In other words, the gain ratio between wave V and wave III is related by Fibonacci to the gain ratio between wave V and wave V$_{20s}$ and between wave V and wave I. (The time ratios are not related by Fibonacci unless we are willing to count a "short" wave V in one ratio and a "long" wave V in the other.) This relationship is not illustrated because of its complexity. Clearly there is more to the market's intricate Fibonacci tapestry than a human mind can even fathom.

### Figure 12-2:

## A $\phi^3$ Price Relationship Between Two of the Grand Supercycle's Impulse Waves

In the 1970s, the Foundation for the Study of Cycles spliced together a number of pre-DJIA stock averages and attached them to the Dow from 1896 to create a continuous index of U.S. stocks from 1789 to the present. For earlier data, the Foundation created the Investment Statistics Index from independent research of reported equity prices (1789-1831) and also used the Cleveland Trust Company Index (1831-1854), the Clement-Burgess Index (1854-1871), the Cowles Commission Index of Industrials (1871-1885) and a Dow Jones index of railroad stocks (1885-1896). (The Foundation also consulted the Hickernell American Insurance Stock Price Averages of 1815-1830 and the Axe-Houghton Industrial Stock Index from 1881 to 1890.)

The accuracy and precision of these earlier aggregations is certainly open to question. In fact, the internal construction of Supercycle wave (III) using these data has always been suggestive of problems in data reliability and consistency. Nevertheless, when we use the Foundation's value for the stock market's low in 1842, we find a Fibonacci relationship.

Two of the Grand Supercycle's impulse waves are related by a power of phi. As you can see in Figure 12-2, Supercycle wave (V) is related to Supercycle wave (III) by $\phi^3$, where $\phi$ = **1.5942**, or approximately **8/5**. In other words, at the January 2000 peak, the Dow Industrial Average not only satisfied myriad Fibonacci relationships to waves dating from the 1990 bottom, the 1987 bottom, the 1982 bottom, the 1974 bottom and the 1932 bottom, but also to the bottom in 1842. The latter two lows occurred in the midst of the two deepest economic depressions of the past two centuries. It is fitting, then, that the top in January 2000 occurred at the peak of the greatest period of optimism in the history of the country. This evidence supports the case from the Elliott wave labels and the time and price relationships in these studies that an extended corrective process lasting perhaps a century will now counterbalance the long bull market that began circa 1784. (For a forecast of its shape, please see Chapter 5 of *At the Crest of the Tidal Wave*.)

Values provided a decade ago by the Foundation for the extremes of waves (I) and (II) were 22.37 and 6.20, respectively. Using those figures, the multiple for wave (III) was 61.47909, whose relationship to wave (V)'s multiple was 1.6662, a virtually perfect **3/2**. Better yet, the resulting multiple of 3.6081 for wave (II) provided an excellent Fibonacci relationship between the corrective waves. Its ratio to wave (IV) was 2.5629, which is $\phi^2$, where $\phi$=1.6009, which is almost exactly **8/5**. Using these figures, two advancing waves and the two corrective waves of the Grand Supercycle formed perfect Fibonacci relationships. Later, the Foundation began reporting new values, the ones used in Figure 12-2. The

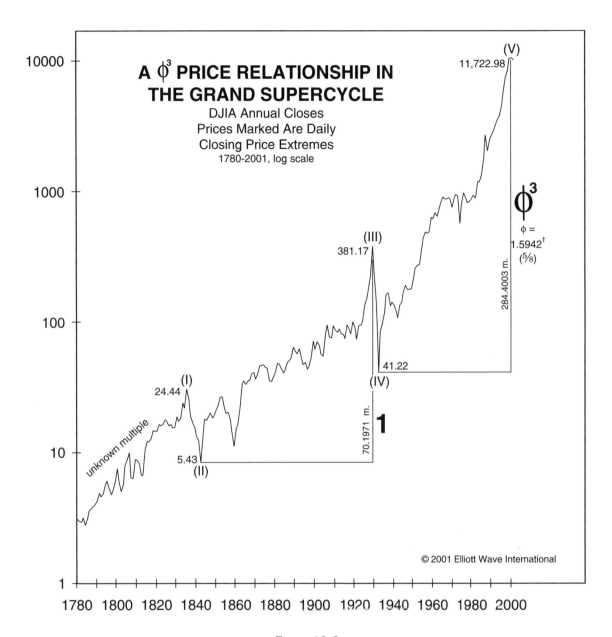

*Figure 12-2*

original values have now been identified as being monthly averages of daily data. While monthly averages are unsuitable for this study, this result is a reminder that our data for the 1800s is not likely precise and that a precise record might have produced different, and possibly better, relationships.

### *Figure 12-3:*

## An Arithmetic Relationship

Elliott came to his conclusion that fifth waves are often related by the Fibonacci ratio to waves one through three upon observing the bull markets of the 1920s and the 1930s, both of which had extended fifth waves. In these cases, wave ⑤ was close to 1.618 times as long as waves ① through ③ in terms of Dow points.

Figure 12-3 shows that there is a fairly close arithmetic relationship of this type within Cycle wave V dating from 1974. If we label the end of wave ④ at the 1991 low (see Figure 4-7), then wave ⑤ is $\phi^3$ times the net travel of waves ① through ③. The multiple is 4.314, close to the limit ratio 4.236 and closer to $(13/8)^3$, which is 4.291. That multiple would have created a top at 11,673.72, which is 49.26 points or 0.42 percent, from the actual high.

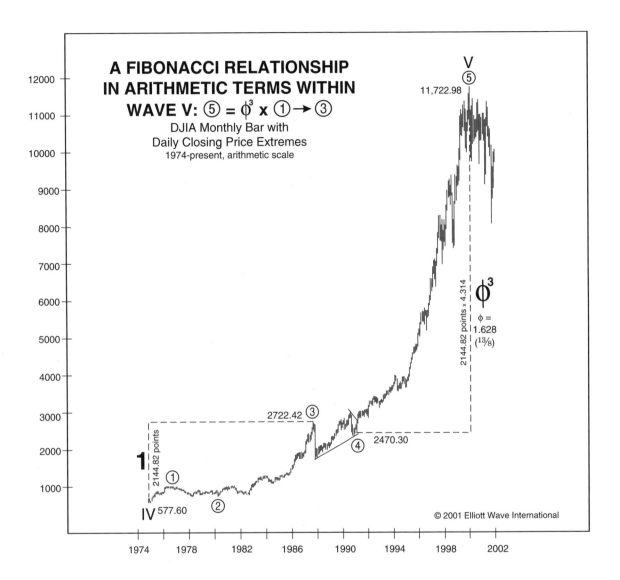

## A FIBONACCI RELATIONSHIP IN ARITHMETIC TERMS WITHIN
## WAVE V: ⑤ = φ³ x ① → ③
DJIA Monthly Bar with
Daily Closing Price Extremes
1974-present, arithmetic scale

*Figure 12-3*

*Figure 12-4:*

## Fourth Wave Affinity?

Chapters 1 and 2 showed that two fifth waves of Cycle degree — wave V of (III) and V of (V) — have substantial affinity. The two related fourth waves may have substantial affinity as well. Wave IV of (III) and wave IV of (V) both take the shape of an expanding triangle when the former is plotted in "constant dollar" terms, i.e., adjusted for the PPI, as shown in Figure 12-4. (For the larger context in which wave (IV) occurs, see Figure 5-4 in *Elliott Wave Principle*.) The third waves of each Supercycle also look similar. Unfortunately, the questionable data of the 19th century precludes a detailed comparison.

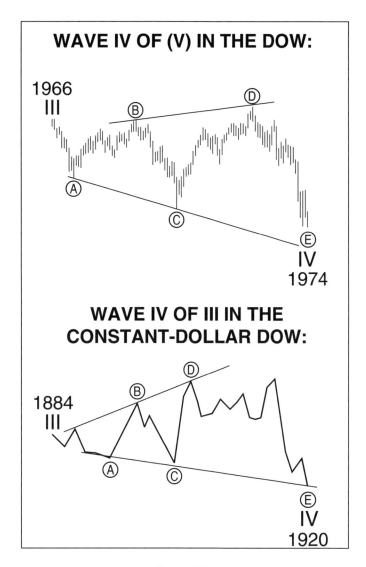

*Figure 12-4*

*Figure 12-5:*

## A Set of Fibonacci Number Multiples

Mr. Jean Comeau of Quebec was briefly cited in another financial newsletter on January 6, 2000 as calling for a Dow top at 11,569. He based his target on the idea of taking the distance of the 1929-1932 decline and multiplying it by the Fibonacci number 34 to get the distance of wave (V). At first glance, it seemed an arbitrary calculation, but Figure 12-5 shows that there is actually a small web of such Fibonacci number multiples. It is not as satisfying as it could be, because while the lows at 2x and 5x skip 3x, and the peaks at 3x and 8x skip 5x, the next peak is not consistent at 21x but occurs near 34x.

To check the validity of the basic idea, I investigated the question of whether either wave II or wave IV led to similar turning points. They did not. This approach, therefore, does not seem to lead to consistently reliable forecasts or form the basis of an Elliott wave guideline. I believe the relationships shown in Figures 3-8, 3-9, 4-2 and 4-3 come closer to describing what is going on in this regard.

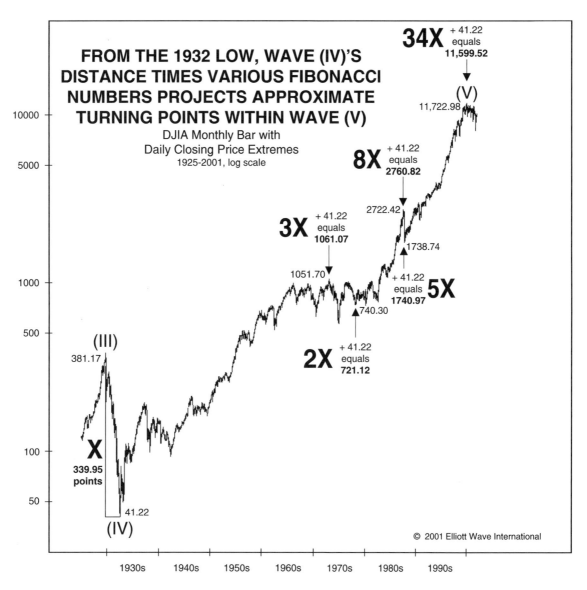

*Figure 12-5*

*Chapter 13*

# *TESTING FOR DATA FITTING*

In order to test whether Elliott's measuring units (wave one, and waves one through three) do in fact have a special value in projecting the ultimate end of a fifth wave or in discovering other wave relationships, I decided to mark four other major distances in the Supercycle to see if they were related by Fibonacci to the previously chosen primary distances, i.e., wave I, waves I-III, and the two main lengths for wave V, which are labeled Y, X, U and T. Figure 13-1 shows the additional multiples P, Q, R and S, which I marked for this purpose.

As it happens, P, R and S have no Fibonacci relationships to each other or to any other marked distance. (See list below.) Q is so small that it has the advantage of high power multiples, yet it provides only one acceptable Fibonacci relationship out of seven possibilities. P/Q is the only "good" ratio out of all 22 possible relationships involving P, Q, R or S. Even then, it sneaks in by a whisker, being off from 2/3 by 0.47 percent, just 0.03 shy of the cutoff point employed in the preceding pages.

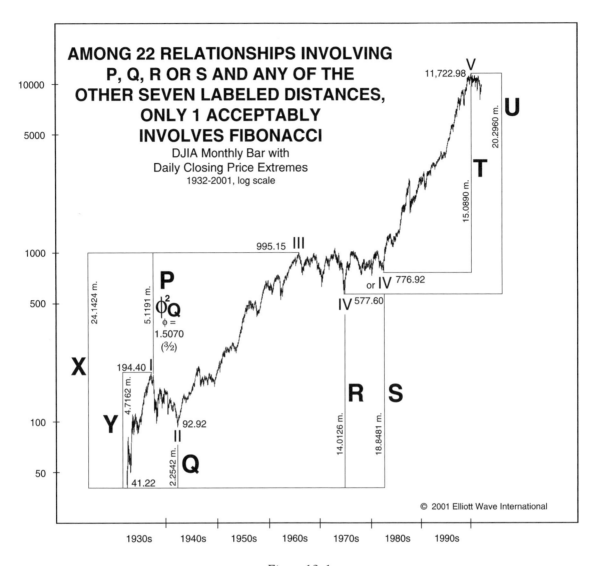

*Figure 13-1*

## No Fibonacci Relationships

P/R = .3653 (near $(3/5)^2$, but not within range)

P/S = .2716

P/T = .3393 (near 1/3, but not within range)

P/U = .2522 (near $(12/19)^3$, but not within range)

P/X = .2120 (near $(2/3)^4$, but not within range)

P/Y = 1.0854

Q/R = .1609

Q/S = .1196 (near $\phi^5$, but not within range)

Q/T = .1494 (near $(18/29)^4$, but not within range)

Q/U = .1111 (near $\phi^5$, but not within range)

Q/X = .0934 (near $(18/29)^5$, but not within range)

Q/Y = .4780

R/S = .7434

R/T = .9287

R/U = .6904

R/X = .5804

R/Y = 2.9712

S/T = 1.2491

S/U = .9287

S/X = .7807

S/Y = 3.996

## Only One Fibonacci Relationship Out of 22 Possibilities

P/Q = 2.2709 ($\phi^2$, where $\phi$ = 1.5070, or 3/2)

There is probably some element of chance in some of the Fibonacci price relationships shown in Chapters 5 through 11, particularly the very few that involve high powers of a Fibonacci ratio. Nevertheless, this brief test demonstrates that deriving Fibonacci relationships is not a matter of simply producing wave values. *Actual* Elliott waves and the one and only multiple-wave "measuring distance" that R.N. Elliott recognized (the net advance of waves one through three) all provide multiples that are related by Fibonacci with striking precision. Multiples *not* involving actual waves fail to do so, even when checked against actual waves and the additional legitimate measuring distance. This is evidence that the Fibonacci relationships detailed in this book are not a matter of data mining but are the natural product of Elliott waves.

Appendices A and C will speak further to this point. They show that charts using a less satisfying starting point for wave V from the standpoint of wave form and those using a percentage method for determining price distance fail to produce anything like the phi-related tapestry displayed in Chapters 2, 6, 7, 9 and 10.

*Postscript*

# A New Perspective on the Quantitative Self-Affinity of Elliott Waves

The stock market is like a tree. Its twigs may be seen as rough replicas of the branches, which may be seen as rough replicas of the whole. But the roughness in the stock market — its supposed "noise" and irregularity — may be only apparent, an artifact of insufficient observation. The preceding studies indicate that various expressions of the Elliott wave fractal, when grouped by their properties of number and extension, and perhaps by degree, have more quantitative similarities than heretofore suspected. If the stock market is truly a robust fractal, then it should display some characteristics of self-identical fractals. Here we have some examples that fill that tall order.

To begin with, we have several impressive examples of waves that expand upon Elliott's observation (see Chapter 3) regarding an extended fifth wave's relationship to the preceding net advance. We have shown that when fifth waves are extended, *wave four — at both its start and its end — marks divisions of the entire impulse wave* that are significant in defining a quantitative affinity — in price and time — with its component fifth wave. Perhaps more important, we have demonstrated that the resulting components of each wave tend to possess the same properties of time and price subdivision, which at least in these cases involve $\phi$, expressed as the Fibonacci ratios 3/5 and 5/8. This striking symmetry may ultimately contribute to explaining why the Dow and S&P indexes rose until precisely the times and prices that they did.

Had an analyst been armed in advance with the knowledge of the approaching point of cross-degree perfection of Figure 11-4, he might have anticipated the end of these concurrently ending multi-year and multi-decade advances to occur on March 24, 2000. The value of these relationships is not only potential and retrospective. An overwhelming consensus has developed that the bear market has ended and that the stock market will achieve new all-time highs soon. If Elliott waves consist of affine fractal components, however, we should conclude the opposite: that the persistent stock market advance of many decades (at least; see Chapter 12) is a completed structure. If it is indeed over, then a correspondingly large bear market is in its infancy. Time will tell which view is correct.

Although I have primarily investigated waves that contain extended fifth waves because those are the ones available in the record, it would make sense that when wave *one* is extended, the Fibonacci time and price divisions of the entire wave would occur at or between the ends of waves one and two. As a preliminary observation, I note that in the case of 1932-1937, a *first* wave that contains an extended fifth wave, wave five lasted 3 out of 5 years, from 1934 to 1937. The subdivision is still Fibonacci, but the longer duration belongs to wave five, not to waves one through four. We will also have to research whether there is a reliable division point when wave *three* is extended.

## Broader Social Implications of the Quantitative Self-Affinity of Elliott Waves

The existence of the Wave Principle means that mass cooperative behavior has form. The preceding chapters show that, compared to its presumed variations, the specificities within that form are more numerous than previously assumed. Some day, someone with a computer will display the entire web of Fibonacci price, time and rate-of-change relationships among these waves, perhaps in one grand formula. The main point to make for now is that Fibonacci ratios appear to govern the stock market's Elliott waves. If so, and if social mood governs the stock market (as *The Wave Principle of Human Social Behavior* contends), then Fibonacci relationships must also govern the entire ebb and flow of social mood.

With this idea in mind, the specific level of the historically low dividend payout at the top in 2000 should not have been so surprising. As we have seen in many of these diagrams, $\phi^2$ is a common price and time relationship between same-numbered waves of one different degree. Turn back to Figure 0-1 to see why this relationship makes sense. The fifth wave in that diagram covers about 38 percent of the entire price range of the wave within which it appears. This ratio, in fact, appears to be the defining relationship relating an impulse wave to its component impulse waves of one lesser degree, providing a new guideline for study and prediction. The 2000 top of Grand Supercycle degree is one degree larger than the 1929 top of Supercycle degree. For the S&P 500, the lowest daily closing yields of 2000 and 1929 respectively were 1.10 and 2.87. The ratio between them is .383, which is off from the ideal limit ratio of $\phi^2$ (.382) by only 1/1000. (Once again, the intraday figures may have produced a perfect limit ratio.) Apparently, not only are waves related by Fibonacci ratios but so also are the measurable extremes of optimism and pessimism at their terminal points. Preliminary data further suggests that the results of these psychological extremes, in terms of social action, manifesting in economic data and war deaths for example, are also related multiplicatively to differences in degree. Fibonacci probably governs far more than stock prices; it probably governs social history in all general aspects.

## Limbic Art

These wonderful pictures prompt a reprise of some commentary I wrote years ago, in 1979, upon observing another multi-year wave structure with unifying properties:

Mathematically speaking, it is much more implausible to argue that these numbers are random or coincidence than it is to accept what is happening, that changes in mass emotions, as reflected by the stock market and most especially the Dow Jones Industrial Average, are tied to certain laws of nature, one of which is best expressed by the Golden Ratio, .618, a mathematical relationship which has been considered one of the great secrets of the universe by, among others, Plato, Pythagoras, Kepler, DaVinci, Newton and the philosopher-mathematician-priests of ancient Egypt.

[The] wave structure I have shown here unfolded its pattern quite clearly regardless of wars, energy crises, speeches, assassinations, Watergates, Peanutgates, jawboning or the weather. To a phenomenal extent, the DJIA appeared to know exactly where it was, exactly where it had been, and exactly where it was going. But *why* is an average of thirty somewhat randomly chosen stocks so reliable in exhibiting over and over again these phenomena of construction?

For a hundred years, investors have noticed that events external to the market often seem to have no effect on the market's progress. With the knowledge that the market continuously unfolds in waves that are related to each other through *form* and *ratio*, we can see why there is little connection. *The market has a life of its own.* Now what ultimately *causes* that particular pattern of the market's life is open to debate. It can be surmised, though, that it is *mass human psychology* that is registering its changes in the barometer known as the DJIA. This idea helps to explain the *cause* of future events: changes in the mass emotional outlook. That's what comes first. The market is a mirror of the forces, whatever they may be, that are affecting humanity both in and out of the market arena. The market doesn't "see into the future" as the discounting idea suggests; it reflects the causes of the future. Increasingly optimistic people expand business; increasingly depressed people contract their businesses. The *results* show up later as a "discounted" future. It's not the politicians who gallantly "save" a bear market by returning to policies of economic sanity, it's the mass emotional environment, as reflected by the market, that forces them at some critical point to do it. Events do not shape the forces of the market; it is the forces behind the market that shape events.

Besides the idea that the emotions of man are tied to the Fibonacci ratio for whatever reason, I think that part of the answer to the Dow's precision lies in the concept of biofeedback. The Dow Industrial Average is the most widely followed market index in the world. It not only *reflects* the pulse of investors, it *affects* the pulse of investors. Not only do our investment decisions force the Dow to go in a certain direction, but the direction of the Dow often causes us to make those very investment decisions. There is a complex emotional involvement there of which we're quite aware but which we don't fully understand. How else can we explain the fact that even though MMM was substituted for Anaconda in the Dow in 1976, the 1976-78 decline still managed to fall exactly to the level that retraced .618 of the 1974-76 advance?[1]

We can bring this conclusion up to date with one additional sentence: Fed meetings are irrelevant to the stock market. This same sentence at some time in the future will be an anachronism. Another update, reflecting the erroneous concerns of that particular time, will undoubtedly have to take its place.

There is a common barrier even to entertaining the idea that the Dow Jones Industrial Average is patterned, which makes some people insist that all of its relationships must be no more than stunning coincidence. They object that the Dow cannot possibly "remember" where it's been or "know" where it is going because it is an internally changing entity. I might glibly reply that the objector himself is an internally changing entity yet he seems to remember where he has been and occasionally to know where he is going. Better, I will offer these comments from *The Wave Principle of Human Social Behavior* (1999):

> Financial markets are a quintessential example of systems whose results feed back into the system as new cause. [E]very market decision is both *produced by* information and *produces* information. Each transaction, while at once an *effect*, becomes part of the market and, by communicating transactional data to investors, joins the chain of *causes* of others' behavior. This process produces a mass feedback loop, which is governed by man's unconscious social nature. Since he *has* such a nature, the process repeatedly generates the same forms.
>
> Stock averages even allow the crowd to monitor itself, like fashion-conscious people watching each other at a shopping mall. In their function as monitors, averages such as the Dow Jones Industrial Average must be maintained as a standard. Let us explore this idea as it relates to the integrity of the DJIA. There is an oft-cited and not unreasonable objection to using the Dow in analysis or forecasting, which is that its components are not constant. For instance, Dow Jones & Co. replaces stocks in its averages from time to time, and occasionally one of the stocks splits. Either event changes the relative weightings of the individual issues in the average. Many people call such changes "distortions," implying that this stock average is a rubber yardstick.
>
> A spokesman for Dow Jones & Co. who maintains the Dow averages, admittedly a partisan on this issue, says, "The components may change with the times, but what the Dow represents remains constant." The precision of the DJIA's long-term wave structures and price relationships over the years supports this view unequivocally.
>
> Investors [must] have a complex emotional relationship with the Dow *as such*, as an entity in itself, much as fans remain loyal to a sports team despite the continual replacement of individual players. Professional investors' actions reflect this loyalty

when they adjust their portfolios after a change in Dow (or S&P) components. They make such adjustments either to mimic what Dow Jones & Co. did or under the assumption that other people will do so. Each of these reasons conforms to the herding impulse.[2]

## Future Fibonacci Relationships

Given the lesson taught by the beautiful pictures in this report, we should expect the Grand Supercycle bear market to exhibit its own Fibonacci relationships. To see how Elliott wave practitioners applied phi to forecast the bottom level for other bear markets, please see pp. 107-109 and Chapter 6 of *The Wave Principle of Human Social Behavior* and their antecedent references.

Should we bet on further Fibonacci relationships among Elliott waves? Sometimes seeming long shots do come in. When they do, it usually means that they weren't actually the long shots that people thought they were. On March 5, 1999, *The Elliott Wave Theorist* reported an example from another field, as reported by a subscriber:

> Fibonacci, a four-year-old colt making his second start in the United States, scored a wire-to-wire upset in the feature race at Santa Anita on February 3. Fibonacci was trained by Derek Meredith, who hadn't had a winner in two years. Fibonacci had won 3 of 8 races in France in 1998 but showed little in his first U.S. start before making every pole a winning one in the one-and-one-eighth mile race over Santa Anita's turf course. Ignored in the betting at 37-1, he returned $76.80 for a $2 win bet.[3]

---

[1] *The Elliott Wave Theorist*, Special Report, August 3, 1979, pp. 8-9

[2] *The Wave Principle of Human Social Behavior*, pp.166-167.

[3] Winograd, Stewart. By letter. Published in *The Elliott Wave Theorist*, March 5, 1999, p. 10.

# APPENDICES

## APPENDIX A

# WAVE RELATIONSHIPS USING WAVE V FROM 1982

Several of the preceding figures (5-11, 6-4, 6-12 and 6-13) show how the entirety of wave V from 1982 and its ①-③ portion are related by Fibonacci both to each other and to portions of the Cycle and Supercycle in both price and time. While these large wave portions participate in Fibonacci relationships, the smaller ones are another story.

The preceding figures that show relationships involving Cycle wave V's first four Primary degree components (waves ①, ②, ③ and ④) all label wave V from the 1974 low. The same types of relationships do not exist in quantity when labeling wave V from 1982. The first three Primary waves by that labeling are much smaller than they are when starting in 1974, and wave ④, while the same size, must relate to a different wave IV, the one ending in 1982.

Figures A-1 through A-7 show what relationships can be gleaned if we try very hard. Among the many possible relationships that *could* have been available, only a few are worth illustrating, and among the eleven near-Fibonacci price decimals shown, only three fall within the established leeway. Cycle wave V forms an excellent Elliott wave trend channel when graphed from the 1974 low, as shown in Figure 18-5 of *The Wave Principle of Human Social Behavior*, Figure 2-6 in Appendix B of *At the Crest of the Tidal Wave*, on page 81 of *View from the Top*, and elsewhere. This appendix serves as further evidence that the starting point for wave V is properly labeled in 1974. Only Figure 5-1 argues eloquently against that conclusion.

### *Figure A-1:*

## Using 1982, the Three Advancing Waves Are Not Well Related by Fibonacci Fractions

Figure A-1 shows how all three Primary-degree advancing waves are related by Fibonacci fractions, using wave ③ as the measuring unit. Neither of these values falls within the acceptable range set forth in Chapter 4. Counting the 1/4 relationship between waves ① and ⑤ as 2/8, which is also $(1/2)^2$, pushes the envelope a bit, though I'm happy to mention it out of pity.

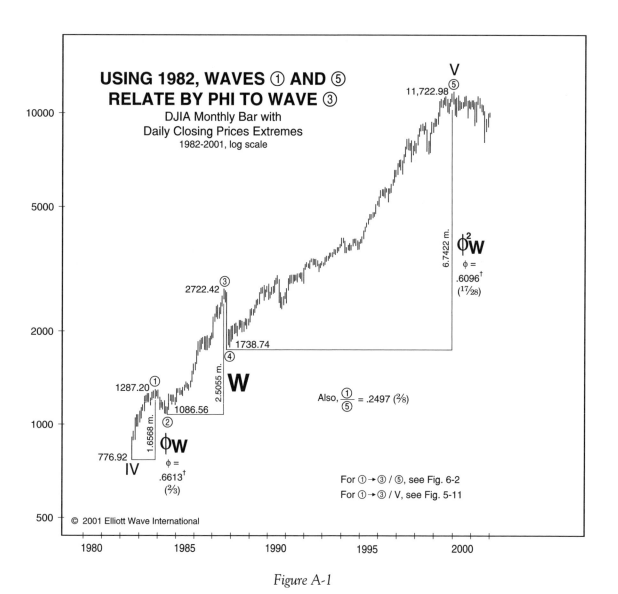

*Figure A-1*

### *Figure A-2:*

## Two Fibonacci Fractions Between Advancing Waves, Using 1982

Waves ① and ③ are related to wave ⑤ from 1990 by 1/3 and 1/2, respectively. Only the 1/3 relationship is within the bounds of our allowed leeway.

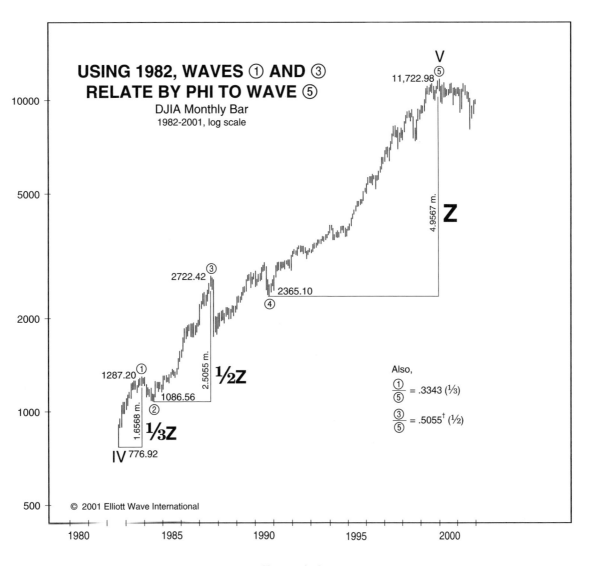

*Figure A-2*

***Figure A-3:***

## Using 1982, the Advancing Waves in Cycle Wave V and the Supercycle Are Not Well Cross-Related by Fibonacci Fractions

Figure A-3 shows how the same type of cross-relationships depicted in Figure 7-1 are also present when labeling wave V as beginning in 1982. However, only ③/III produces a ratio with an acceptable Fibonacci root, as .2339 is $\phi^3$, where $\phi$ = .6161 (8/13).

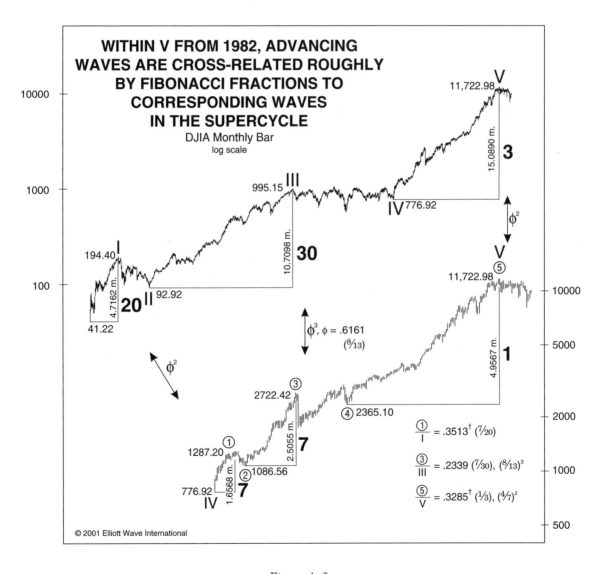

Figure A-3

### Figure A-4:

## Using 1982, Corrections Are *Not* Satisfactorily Related by Phi

Figure 7-2 shows that the corrections within the Cycle and Supercycle are cross-related by Fibonacci when starting wave V in 1974. When starting wave V in 1982, the corrections are *not* cross-related by Fibonacci. The multiples of waves ② and II are related by .5663, which is close to 4/7, a "Fibonacci" ratio that, along with 1/2, lies outside the range of most Fibonacci number fractions. Wave IV by this interpretation is so small that no smaller multiple could create a Fibonacci fraction! Turning to the percentage difference between the ending and starting points, we find a "Fibonacci" fraction of .3635, which is almost exactly 4/11 and fairly close to $(3/5)^2$.

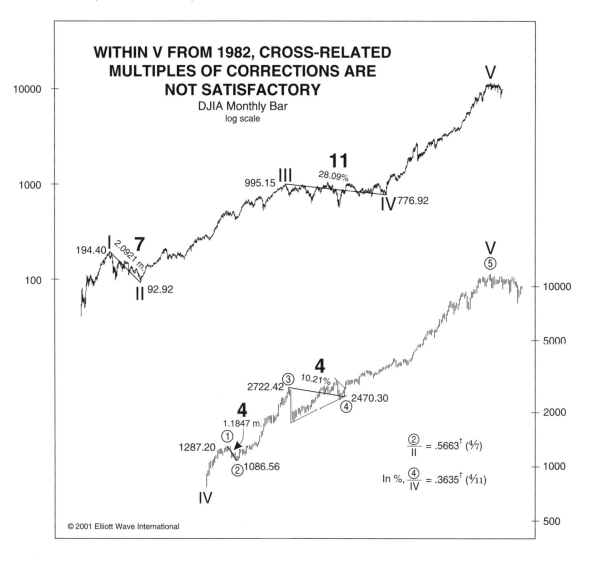

Figure A-4

## *Figure A-5:*

## Using 1982, All Advancing Waves Last A Fibonacci Number of Years

This is the cousin of Figure 9-1, but it is not as satisfying because the adjacent durations do not form identically spaced Fibonacci fractions.

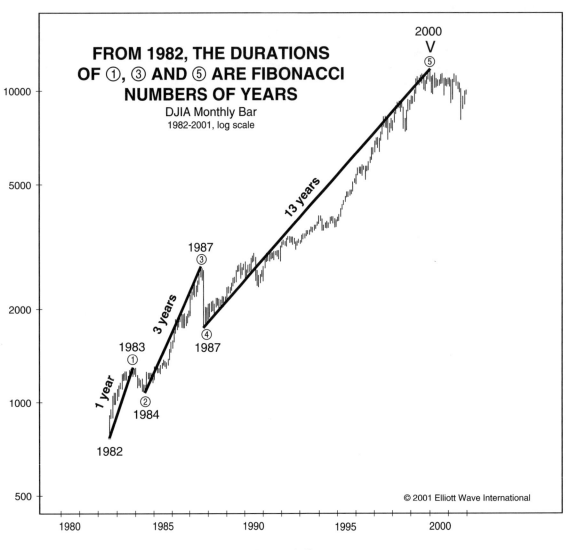

Figure A-5

### Figure A-6:

## Using 1982, All Durations in Years Are Cross-Related to the Supercycle by Fibonacci Number Ratios

The market's option of ending wave ④ in 1991 makes all durations in years cross-related by fractions that employ Fibonacci numbers. Most of the fractions, however, are not powers of phi. Only 5/34 is an acceptable power of phi, where $\phi$ = .6193, approximately 13/21. This picture, however, does not hold a candle to the elegance of Figure 10-1.

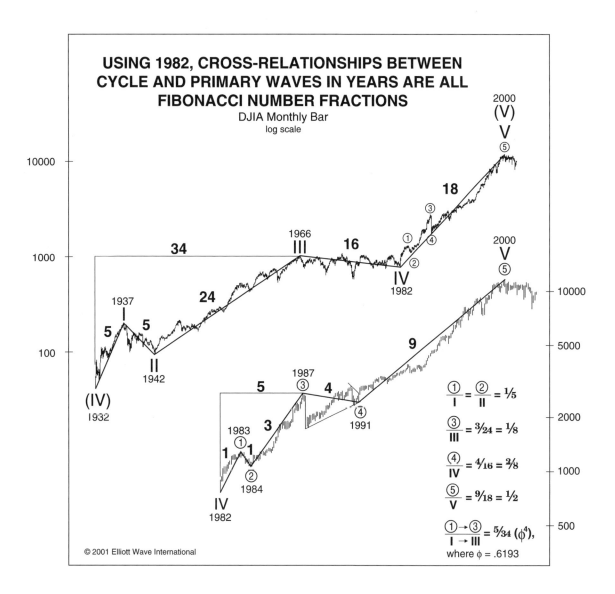

Figure A-6

*Figure A-7:*

## Using 1982, the First Waves Are Cross-Related by $\phi^3$ in Terms of Days, but the Second, Third and Fourth Waves Are Not Cross-Related By Fibonacci

When counting wave V from 1982, wave ① has two acceptable ending points: its price high in September 1983 and its orthodox top in January 1984. When a cross-relationship between waves ① and I produced the ratio .2374, which is within one day of 5/21 and within two days of a .236 relationship, I thought there was a chance that all the other waves would also produce Fibonacci relationships. In fact, there are no acceptable phi relationships between waves ② and II, ③ and III, ④ and IV or ⑤ and V. This is despite two acceptable ending dates for wave ③, four acceptable ending dates for wave ④ and three acceptable ending dates for wave ⑤ (and therefore V)! Perhaps it is a good thing that we can derive only a single Fibonacci relationship from these 21 acceptable combinations of durations because it serves to show that it is not easy to manipulate the figures to produce the startling relationships outlined in the main section of this book.

For an idea of the kind of multiples produced, peruse this list of durations and ratios available for wave ⑤ as they relate to the corresponding durations for wave V, in days:

| | |
|---|---|
| 10/19/98 - 1/14/00 | 4470 / 6364 = .7024 |
| 10/19/87 - 3/24/00 | 4540 / 6434 = .7056 |
| 10/19/87 - 9/6/00 | 4706 / 6600 = .7130 |
| 12/4/87 - 1/14/00 | 4424 / 6364 = .6952 |
| 12/4/87 - 3/24/00 | 4494 / 6434 = .6985 |
| 12/4/87 - 9/6/00 | 4660 / 6600 = .7061 |
| 10/11/90 - 1/14/00 | 3382 / 6364 = .5314 |
| 10/11/90 - 3/24/00 | 3452 / 6434 = .5365 |
| 10/11/90 - 9/6/00 | 3618 / 6600 = .5482 |
| 1/9/91 - 1/14/00 | 3292 / 6364 = .5173 |
| 1/9/91 - 3/24/00 | 3362 / 6434 = .5225 |
| 1/9/91 - 9/6/00 | 3528 / 6600 = .5345 |

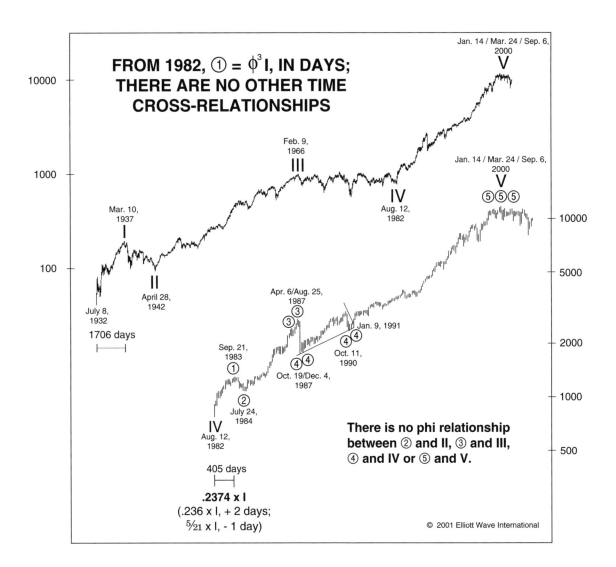

Figure A-7

# WAVE RELATIONSHIPS USING WAVE V FROM 1980

The contrast between the results obtained in Appendix A and those in the main portion of this book helps address the question as to which low (1974 or 1982) best accommodates the Wave Principle. By almost all price and time relationships among relevant waves, the 1974 low is more compelling than the 1982 low, which supports the superior case for 1974 in terms of wave form.

Figures 5-13 and 6-12 display measurements that utilize the 1980 low for the end of wave IV. This appendix explores the price and time relationships among relevant waves under that assumption.

There are two points that may be labeled the end of wave IV in 1980 on a daily closing basis: March 27 (the day of the intraday low) at 759.98 (for the record, the closing price was the same on March 28) and April 21, on which day the closing low occurred at 759.13. These turns are nearly identical in price, so they make little difference in the calculations. In these illustrations, I use whichever price point edges the ratios closer to ideal values. For time calculations, the only date that produces meaningful relationships is March 27.

Three points may be labeled the high of wave ①: two acceptable orthodox tops, at 966.72 on August 15, 1980 and 1000.17 on November 20, 1980, and the price high at 1024.05 on April 27, 1981. The first two peaks provide no Fibonacci price relationships, so the price high is the only one featured in these illustrations. Figure B-8 uses the earliest peak for a time relationship.

Many wonderful wave relationships disappear when labeling wave IV in 1980. There is no Fibonacci relationship between waves I and V, ② and ④ or V and (V), no arithmetic relationship between waves ①-③ and ⑤, and no Fibonacci time relationships in days among Primary waves involving waves ①, ② or ①-③. There is an 11/18 relationship (1.2735/2.0921) between waves ② and II, which would be worth showing if there were any cross-relationships between any of the other waves, but there aren't. Needless to say, the duration of each entire wave no longer splits into Fibonacci proportion at the low of wave four or in half at the peak of wave three. Figure 6-12 shows two relationships that remain valid when using the 1980 low for wave IV, although they then would no longer both apply to wave ③ but rather individually to wave ③ and waves ①-③.

Finding Fibonacci relationships under this wave labeling is like pulling teeth from a donkey. (Not that I have any first-hand experience, although I do run a business and occasionally trade markets.) Among the few relationships worth mentioning, only a few fall inside the narrow bounds adopted for a convincing Fibonacci relationship, as you will see in the following pages.

### Figure B-1:

## The Relationship to Waves I-III Is Not As Good

Using the 1980 low, wave V has an approximate Fibonacci relationship to waves I-III. The relationship shown in Figure 5-1 is far more satisfying.

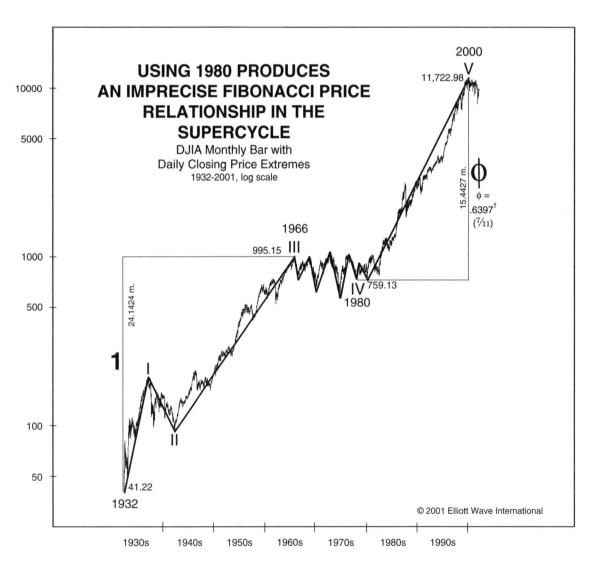

Figure B-1

## *Figure B-2:*

## Still a Relationship between Waves II and IV

Using the 1980 low, wave IV is .6259 times wave II, which is close to **5/8** and thus better than the ratio shown in Figure 5-10.

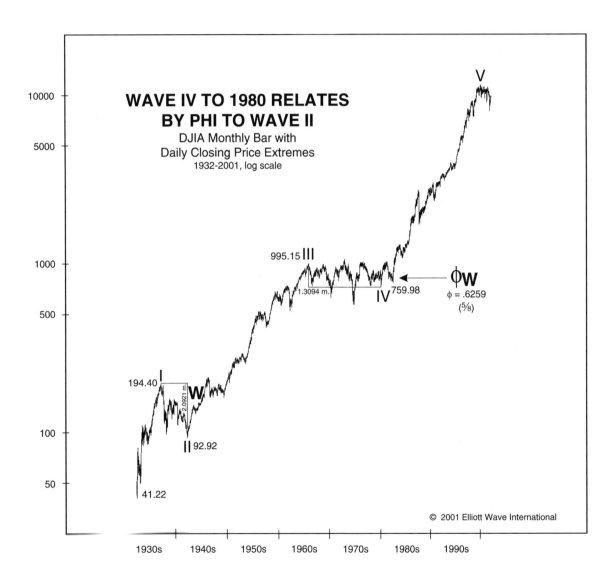

*Figure B-2*

## Figure B-3:

## Two Relationships at (8/13)$^6$

Using the 1980 low, wave V is $(8/13)^6$ times (V), as first shown in Figure 5-13, and wave IV is $(8/13)^6$ times I-III. Both ratios are exact to six decimal places, at .054299! As I cannot see a reason for this match in terms of wave form, it may be coincidence. The decimal is also close to 3/55.

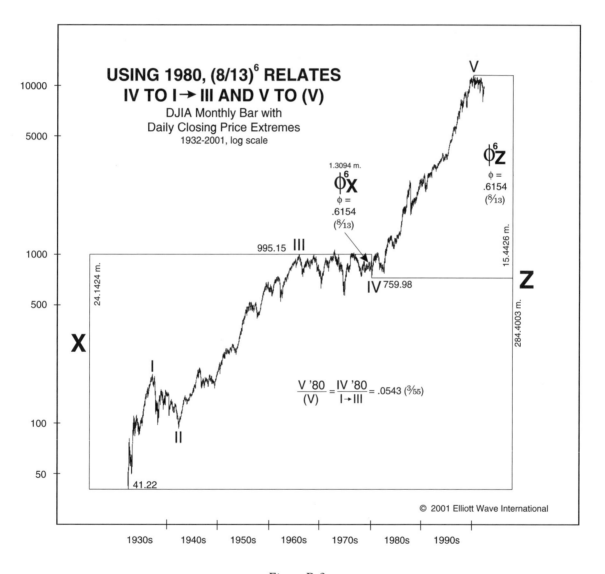

*Figure B-3*

### *Figure B-4:*

### Using the 1980 Low, the Wave One Measuring Unit Is Related by Fibonacci Fractions to Waves ③, ①-③ and ⑤.

The title sounds good, and the ratios are nearly exact at 2.6004 (13/5), 2.6584 (8/3) and 5.0035 (5/1). Yet the ratios depicted here have little to do with each other, so they do not present a very interesting picture.

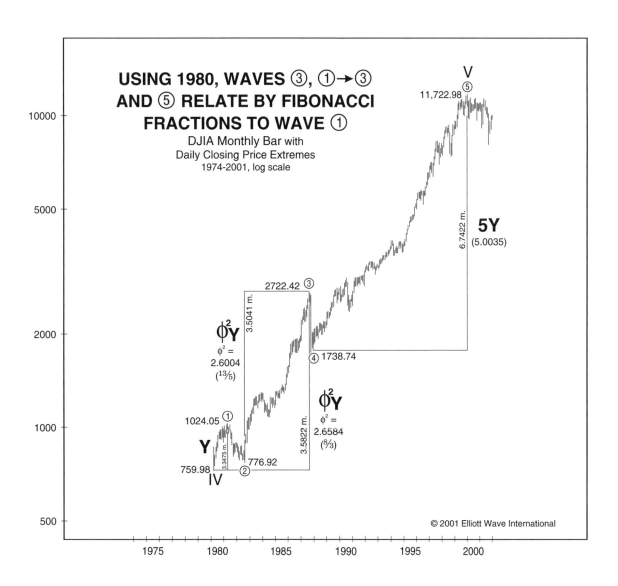

Figure B-4

***Figure B-5:***

## Fibonacci Durations in Years

Beginning at the 1980 low, wave V still progressed via three advances each lasting a Fibonacci number of years, as occurs using the 1982 low in Figure A-5. The Fibonacci number alternation that enhances Figure 9-1, however, is absent.

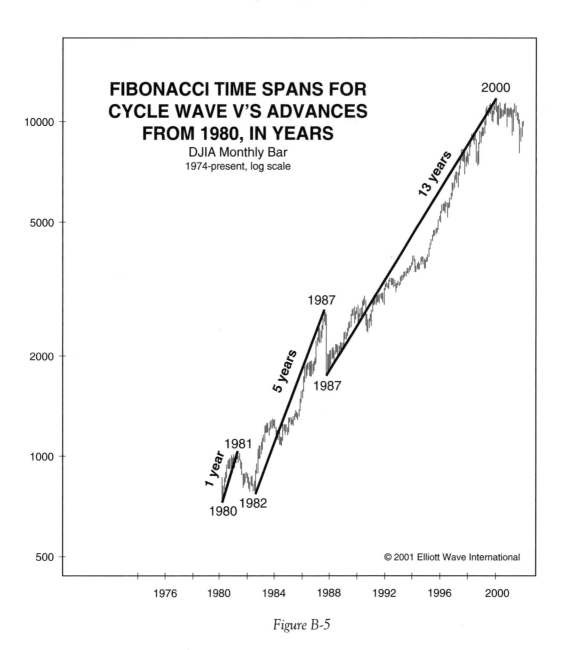

*Figure B-5*

**Figure B-6:**

## Time Cross-Relationships

Shifting the low of wave IV to 1980, remarkably, does not eliminate time cross-relationships. Nor, however, does it come close to its impressive layout of Figure 10-1. To squeeze regularity from the picture, I have to cheat a bit and use 1967 as a compromise year denoting the top of wave III, which is between the Dow's orthodox top in 1966 and the final high in the Value Line and Amex indexes in 1968. Upon doing so, we find that waves one through four of the Cycle and the Supercycle (and their various combinations and totals) each have a 1/5 relationship to each other. The fifth waves have a 1/2 relationship. The fifth waves could not have produced a 1/5 relationship because it would have required a top between 1992 and 1993.

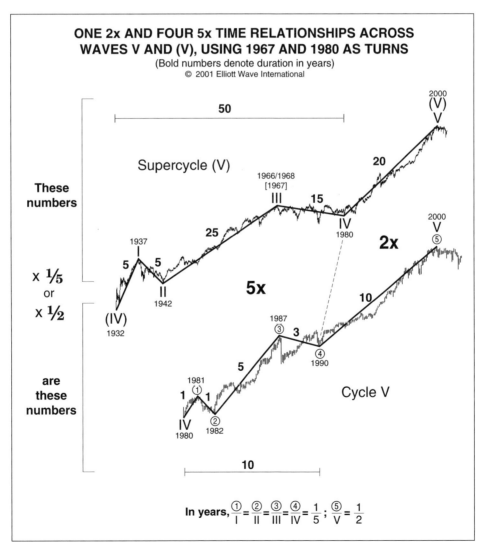

*Figure B-6*

## *Figure B-7:*

## Two Time Cross-Relationships between Advancing Waves

The first waves still have a Fibonacci cross-relationship when using the 1980 low as the end of wave IV. The fifth waves have an excellent relationship, as wave ⑤ from December 1987 is only 8 days shy of being .618 times the duration of wave V. This pairing uses the 1987 and 1980 lows, while the one in Figure 10-2 uses the 1990 and 1974 lows. These two relationships of $\phi$ and $\phi^2$ seem to "explain" why the market made all four turns. The third waves have no Fibonacci relationship.

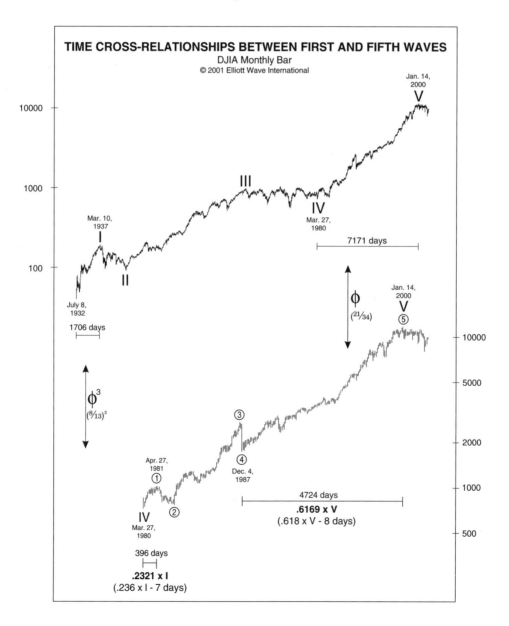

*Figure B-7*

## Figure B-8:

## Cross-Relationships between Corrective Waves

Both sets of corrective waves have approximate Fibonacci cross-relationships, although neither one of them falls within the acceptable leeway. To get a relationship between the second waves requires using the date of the orthodox top on August 15, 1980 for wave ①. This requirement is less than satisfactory given that the time relationship between the first waves in Figure B-7 requires the top to be labeled on April 27, 1981. Nor are the powers consistent (as they are in Figure 10-4), since in this case one is $\phi^2$ and the other is $\phi^3$.

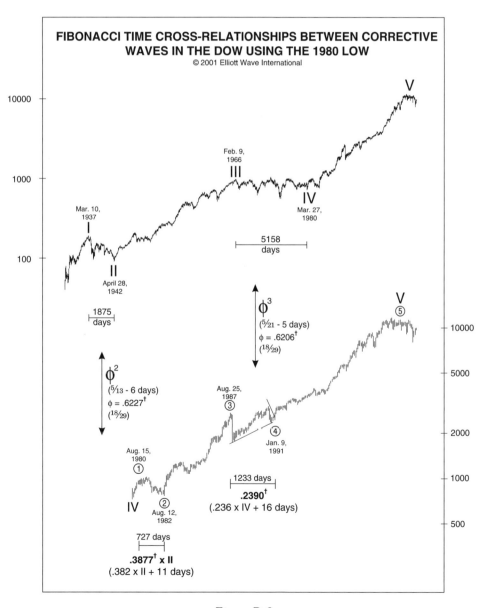

Figure B-8

# WAVE RELATIONSHIPS IN PERCENTAGE TERMS

To test my conclusion that multiples are more accurate representatives of market relationships than percentage gains, I reviewed all the charts in Chapters 5, 6 and 7 and recalculated their relationships in percentage terms. I chose among the available values for termination points whenever possible, such as those for wave IV, ③ and ④, to try to make them work out. The most glaring failure of the percentage gains was in relating the waves of Supercycle (V) to Cycle wave V. Figures 7-3 and 7-4 cannot be recast using percentages. In other words, if percentage gains were all we had to work with, we would not know that these waves were cross-related both in their entireties and between their related components. Because the components of wave V and (V) are so closely related in terms of form, as we saw in Chapter 2, we might expect them to be cross-related quantitatively by Fibonacci number relationships. They are, but those relationships turn up only when using multiples.

Percentage gains fail to provide the symmetry and elegance of the illustrations in Chapters 5, 6 and 7, despite opportunity for manipulation. Of the 28 relationships deemed worthy of illustration, only 12 fall within the established leeway.

## Figure C-1:

### Wave V From 1982, in %

As we saw in Chapter 3, in terms of percentage gain, wave V from 1982 is .6088 times the net travel of waves I-III. This ratio is not within the acceptable ranges. Using the 1980 low for wave IV, the ratio is 1444.27%/2314.24%, which is .6241. This decimal is close to 5/8, yet this result pales in comparison to the perfection of Figure 5-1.

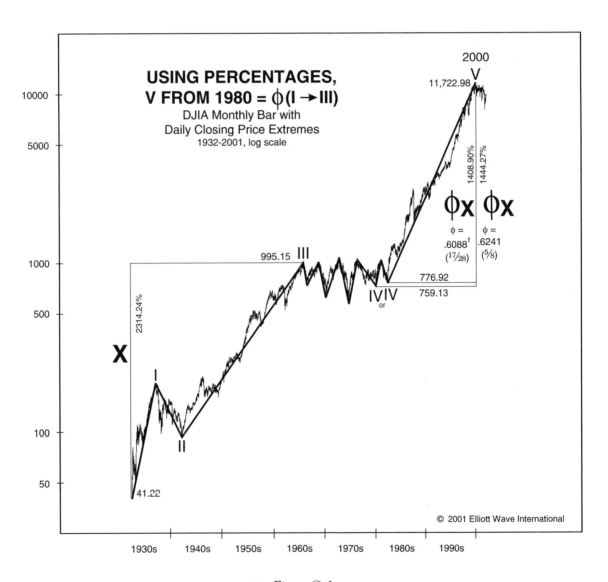

Figure C-1

## Figure C-2:

### Wave V From 1974, in %

When using percentage gains, wave V is still related to wave I by phi, but in this case, it requires $\phi^4$ rather than $\phi^3$. The ratio (1.5095) is close to 3/2 but outside our established range and not nearly as close as the 13/8 fraction shown in Figure 5-3. This is despite the "fudge factor" being larger when raising a range to a higher power. Using the 1980 low for wave IV does not help. In that case, the ratio is 1444.27%/371.62%, which is 3.8864, or $\phi^3$, where $\phi$ = 1.5723 (11/7).

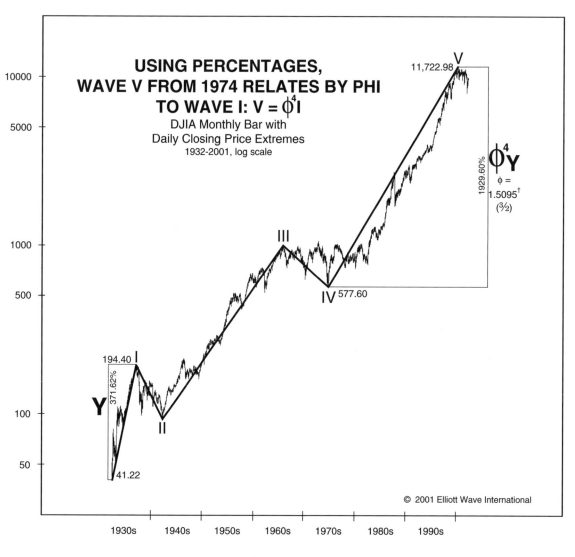

*Figure C-2*

**Figure C-3:**

## In %, Each Measuring Wave Relates to the Entire Supercycle

Waves I-III are related to the entire Supercycle by $\phi^5$, where $\phi = 1.6504$, which is outside our acceptable range for a Fibonacci ratio. This particular wave relationship is no better than that produced by multiples in Figure 5-6.

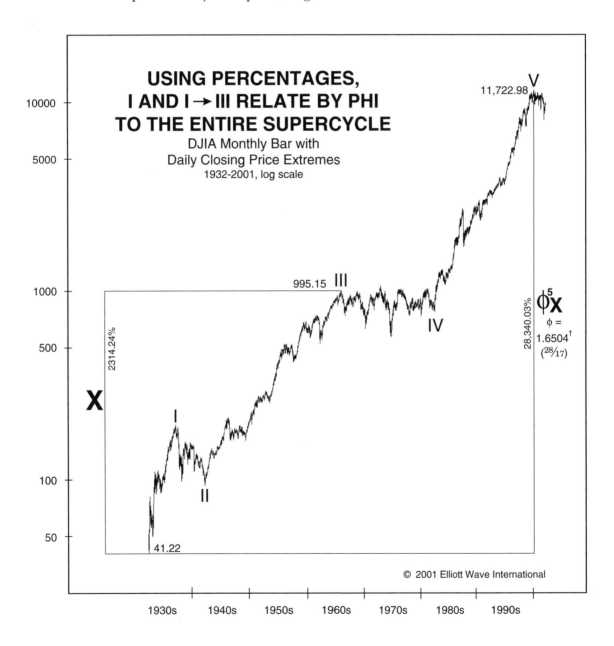

*Figure C-3*

## *Figure C-4:*

## In %, Wave III Relates with Uneven Success to Four Other Distances

Figure 5-7 establishes that when using price multiples, each primary measuring unit is related to wave III by $\phi^2$, where phi is 3/2 and 2/3, respectively. When using percentage gains, no such symmetry emerges. Nor is the relationship between wave III and wave ⑤ as successful. Figure C-4 shows what I can come up with.

Although Figure 5-7 presents a much more elegant picture than Figure C-4, there is one notable relationship when using percentage gains. As *The Elliott Wave Theorist* noted many years ago, the percentage gain of wave III is 2.616 times the percentage gain of wave I, a nearly perfect $\phi^2$ limit ratio (see Figure C-5). Because of this relationship and that in Figure C-3, there is also a phi relationship between waves III and (V), but is requires a very high power of seven.

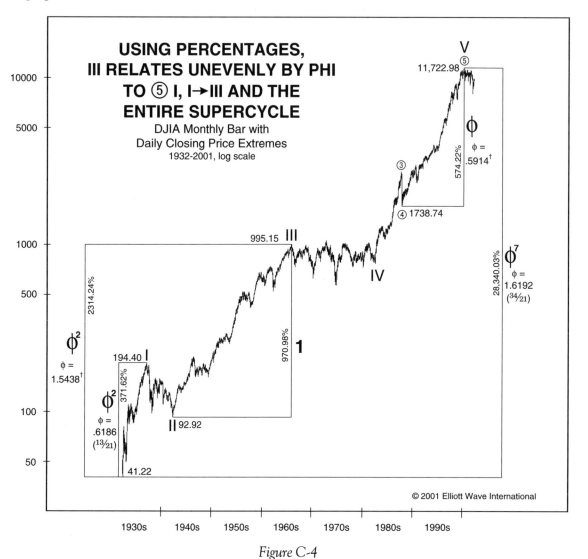

*Figure C-4*

## *Figure C-5:*

## Combining the Two Best Phi-Based Percentage Relationships

Figure C-5 combines the only two "good" relationships from Figures C-1 through C-4, using the standard measuring units. Figure C-5 is our blue ribbon picture using percentage gains.

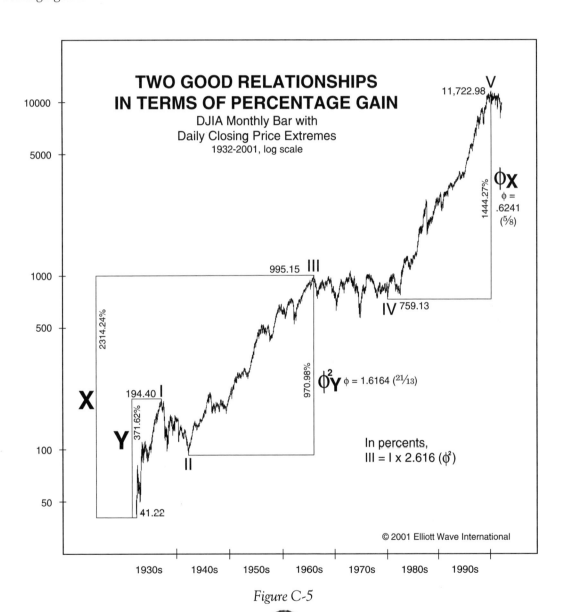

Figure C-5

## Figure C-6:

### Relationships Between the Corrections and Wave I, in %

In Figure 5-10, wave IV from *1982* is φII when using multiples. In this figure, wave IV from *1974* is φII when using percentage gains. (To get the value of the range for the correction, the percentage difference is measured from low to high, not as a percentage loss from high to low.)

The Fibonacci roots for the relationships among the multiples for waves I, II and IV all approximate 2/3. Those involving wave I fall within our acceptable ranges.

These lengths also relate by Fibonacci arithmetically, in terms of points traveled. Wave II at 101.48 points and wave I at 153.18 points are related by .6626, also approximately 2/3. Wave II and wave IV (to 1974) at 417.55 points are related by $\phi^3$, where $\phi$ = .6241 (5/8). Waves I and IV are related by $\phi^2$, where $\phi$ = .6057. Wave IV to 1982 does not relate by Fibonacci to these other two waves in terms of points, although in percentage terms, wave IV to 1982 is related to wave II by .257, approximately 2/8. These relationships are not shown in Figure C-6.

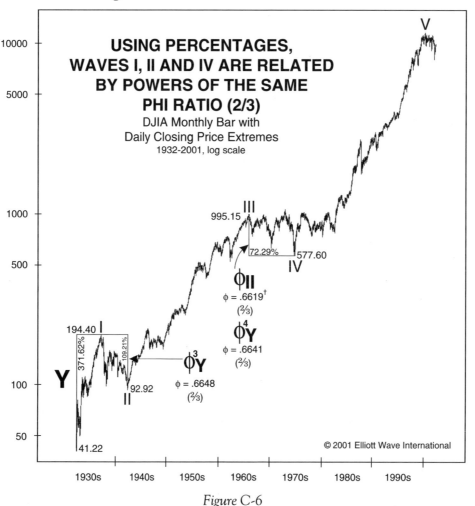

*Figure C-6*

### Figure C-7:

### Wave V to the 1987 High, in %

This picture is interesting in terms of percentage gains, because the distance labeled Z is fairly close to 2/3 of the distance labeled Y. For this reason, wave V from 1974 is related to both of those distances (Y and Z) by phi to a power, where phi is quite close to 3/2.

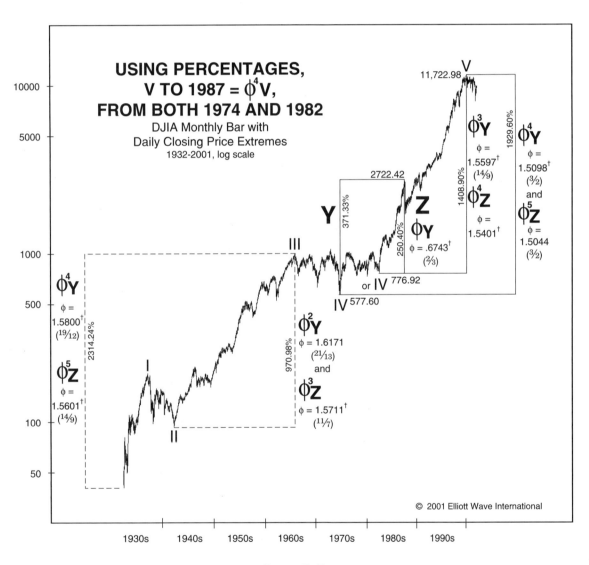

*Figure C-7*

*Figure C-8:*

## Relating Wave (V) to Its Motive Sub-waves, in %

It was interesting to find that in percentage terms, waves I and III relate to wave (V) by powers of essentially the same decimal, which is .6177 ±.0001, a nearly perfect expression of φ. Nine is the highest power illustrated in this book, which reduces the importance of this equivalence, but what really mars the picture is that despite three starting points and two powers to choose from, wave V has no Fibonacci relationship to wave (V) that comes anywhere near the spread allowed for any of our Fibonacci number fractions.

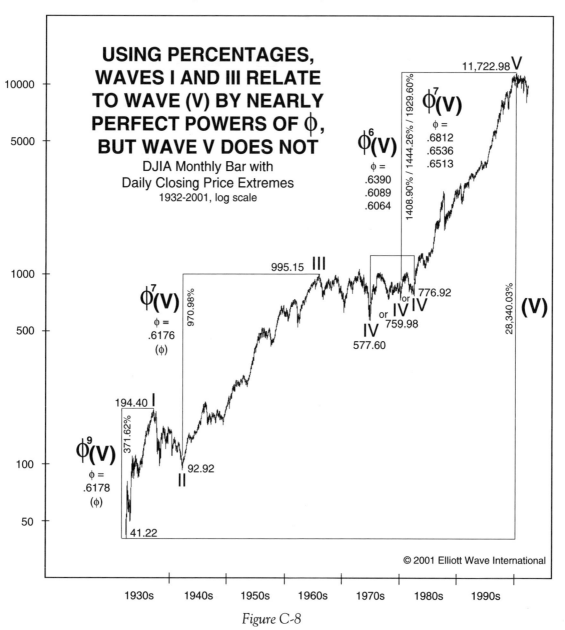

*Figure C-8*

### Figure C-9:

### In %s, the Smaller and Larger Versions of Waves Produce Similar Multiples

Figure 6-3 shows excellent Fibonacci relationships between both the smaller and larger versions of waves ①–③ and wave ⑤. When converting the distances to percentage gains, interesting relationships show up not between the two smaller versions and the two larger versions, but between the smaller version and the larger version of each distance. The relationship is to a single power of phi, where $\phi = 1.52 \pm .01$. This is an interesting set of relationships, though the ratios fall outside our acceptable ranges for Fibonacci fractions.

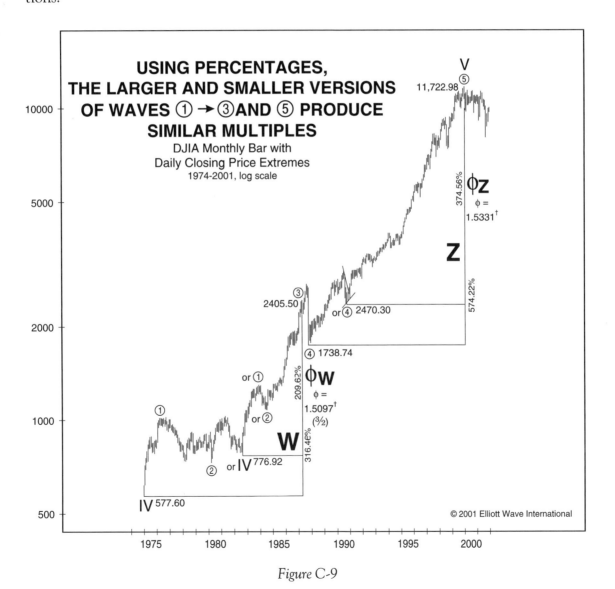

Figure C-9

**Figure C-10:**

## Using %s, Wave ⑤ is in $\phi^4$ Relationship to Wave ①

Wave ① has two ending points: the price extreme of 1014.79 and the orthodox top at 1004.65. Using the latter, the percentage gain of wave ⑤ is 1.6694 (5/3) times that of wave ①. This figure is just as satisfying as Figure 6-7.

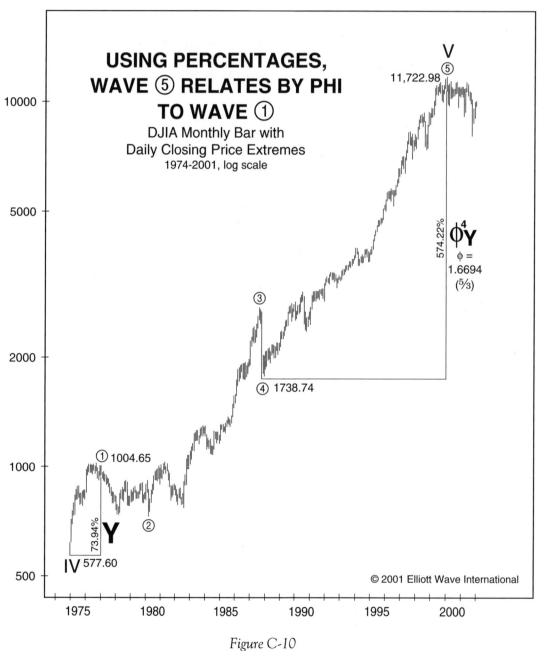

Figure C-10

(corresponds to 6-7)

### Figure C-11:

In this figure, two distances for wave ③ and two distances for wave ⑤, expressed in percentage gains, yield Fibonacci relationships. This fairly interesting chart corresponds to Figure 6-12. As in Figure C-1, the 1980 low produces an acceptable percentage-based relationship.

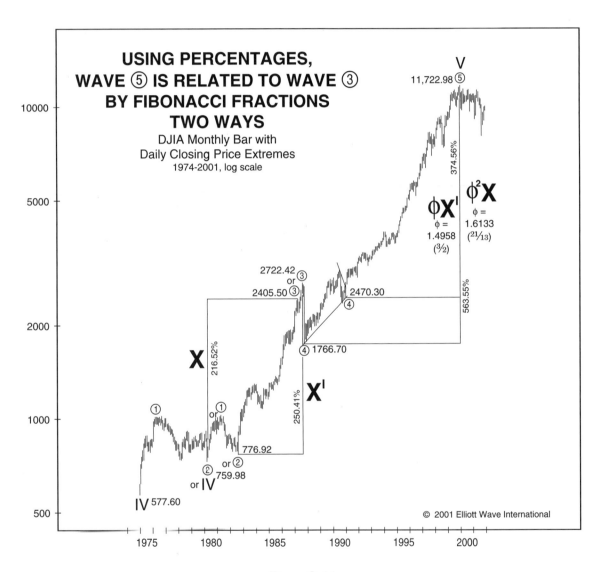

Figure C-11

## *Figures C-12:*

## A Set of Relationships in Percentage Terms

As already mentioned, *The Elliott Wave Theorist* noted years ago that in percentage terms waves I and III are virtually perfectly related via $\phi^2$. I also noted that the percentage gains are actually multiples of phi, so that given $\phi = 161.8\%$, then wave I = 6/$\phi$, and wave III = 6$\phi$. Now we find that measuring from the 1974 low, wave V is fairly close to 12$\phi$, which is twice the multiple of wave III. The actual high in the DJIA is off from the ideal projection by 71 points, just 0.6%.

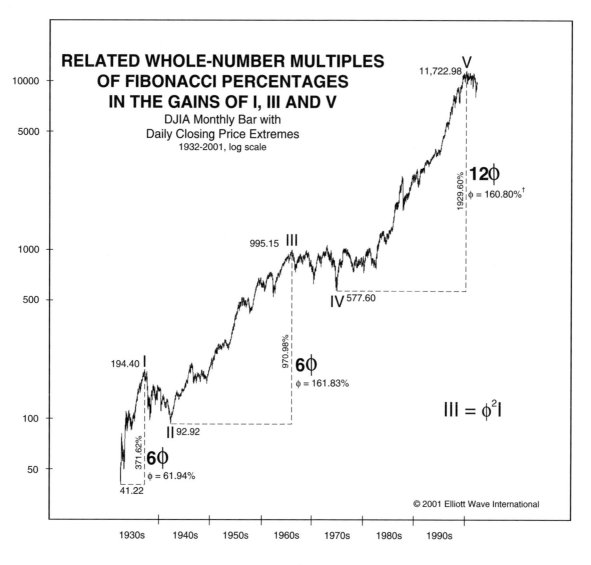

*Figure C-12*

## Figure C-13:

### The Same Percentage Relationships, Expressed in Terms of Wave III

The wave relationships in Figure C-13 are the same as those in Figure C-12 except that they are expressed in both additive and multiplicative relationships to wave III. In these cases, $\phi$ is nearly the ideal limit ratio, at .6180 ± .0007.

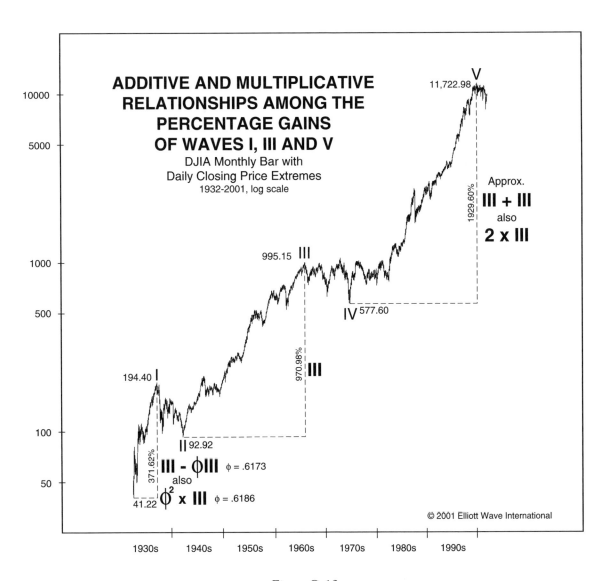

Figure C-13

## TABLE C-A: LIST OF VALUES SHOWN IN THE
## ILLUSTRATIONS IN APPENDICES A, B AND C

Numbers in parentheses are the fractions that the preceding decimals approach.

Numbers in bold denote percentages away from perfect Fibonacci number fractions. (.09 means 0.09 percent, not 9 percent.)

Italic numbers to the right in each box indicate the power of the phi root. 1- $\phi$ expressions within tolerance for $\phi$ are marked to the first power.

The symbol † indicates ratios outside the narrow limits listed in Tables 4-F, 4-G, 4-I and 4-J.

| Figure | Values | Power |
|---|---|---|
| Figure A-1 | 0.6613† (2/3) **.81** | 1 |
| | 0.6096† (17/28) **.41** | 2 |
| | 0.2497 (2/8) **.12** | 2 |
| Figure A-2 | 0.3343 (1/3) **.30** | 1 |
| | 0.5055† (1/2) **1.10** | 1 |
| Figure A3 | 0.3513† (3/5)² **1.20** | 1 |
| | 0.2339 (7/30) **.26** [(8/13)² **.11**] | 3 |
| | 0.3285† (4/7)² **.30** [(1/3) **1.44**] | 1 |
| Figure A-4 | 0.5663† (4/7) **.89** | 1 |
| | 0.3635† (4/11) **.03** [(3/5)² **.48**] | 1 |
| Figure A-5 | 1/3 **0**, 3/13 **0** | 1 3 |
| Figure A-6 | 1/5 **0**, 1/8 **0**, 2/8 **0**, 1/2 **0** | 3 4 3 1 |
| | 0.6193 (13/21) **.03** | 4 |
| Figure A-7 | 0.2374 (5/21) **.29** | 3 |
| Figure B-1 | 0.6397† (7/11) **.52** | 1 |
| Figure B-2 | 0.6259 (5/8) **.14** | 1 |
| Figure B-3 | repeat | |
| | 0.6154 (8/13) **0** | 6 |
| Figure B-4 | 2.6004 (13/5) **.02** | 1 |
| | 2.6584 (8/3) **.31** | 1 |
| | 5.0035 (5/1) **.07** | 3 |
| Figure B-5 | 1/5 **0**, 5/13 **0** | 3 1 |
| Figure B-6 | 1/5 **0**, 1/5 **0**, 1/5 **0**, 1/5 **0**, 1/2 **0** | 3 3 3 3 1 |
| Figure B-7 | 0.2321 (8/13)³ **.13** | 3 |
| | 0.6169 (21/34) **.13** | 1 |
| Figure B-8 | 0.3877† (5/13) **.81** [(18/29)² **.32**] | 1 |
| | 0.2390† (5/21) **.34** [(18/29)³ **.04**] | 3 |
| Figure C-1 | 0.6088† (17/28) **.28** | 1 |
| | 0.6241 (5/8) **.14** | 1 |
| Figure C-2 | 1.5095† (3/2) **.63** | 4 |
| Figure C-3 | 1.6504† (28/17) **.21** | 5 |
| Figure C-4 | 1.5438† (11/7) **1.76** | 2 |
| | 0.6186 (13/21) **.08** | 2 |
| | 0.5914 (3/5)† **1.43** | 1 |
| | 1.6192 (34/21) **.01** | 7 |

| Figure | Values | Power |
|---|---|---|
| Figure C-5 | repeats | |
| Figure C-6 | 0.6648 (2/3) **.28** | 3 |
| | 0.6619† (2/3) **.72** | 1 |
| | 0.6641 (2/3) **.39** | 4 |
| Figure C-7 | 1.5800† (19/12) **.21** | 4 |
| | 1.5601† (14/9) **.30** | 5 |
| | 1.6171 (21/13) **.11** | 2 |
| | 1.5711† (11/7) **.02** | 3 |
| | 0.6743† (2/3) **1.14** | 1 |
| | 1.5597† (14/9) **.27** | 3 |
| | 1.5401† (14/9) **.99** | 4 |
| | 1.5098† (3/2) **.65** | 4 |
| | 1.5044 (3/2) **.29** | 5 |
| Figure C-8 | 0.6178 ($\phi$) **.03** | 9 |
| | 0.6176 ($\phi$) **.06** | 7 |
| | 0.6390 (7/11) **.41** | 6 |
| | 0.6089 (17/28) **.30** | 6 |
| | 0.6064 (17/28) **.12** | 6 |
| | 0.6812 (2/3) **2.17** | 7 |
| | 0.6536 (9/14) **1.67** | 7 |
| | 0.6513 (9/14) **1.31** | 7 |
| Figure C-9 | 1.5097† (3/2) **.65** | 1 |
| | 1.5331† (14/9) **1.44** | 1 |
| Figure C-10 | 1.6694 (5/3) **.16** | 4 |
| Figure C-11 | 1.4958 (3/2) **.28** | 1 |
| | 1.6133 (21/13) **.13** | 1 |
| Figure C-12 | 61.94% (13/21) **.02** | 1 |
| | 161.83% ($\phi$) **.02** | 1 |
| | 160.80% (29/18) **.19** | 1 |
| Figure C-13 | 0.6173 (21/34) **.06** | 1 |
| | 0.6186 (13/21) **.08** | 1 |

*Table C-A*

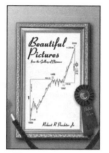

 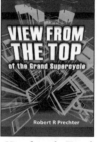 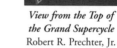